Picturing Black New Orleans

UNIVERSITY PRESS OF FLORIDA

Florida A&M University, Tallahassee
Florida Atlantic University, Boca Raton
Florida Gulf Coast University, Ft. Myers
Florida International University, Miami
Florida State University, Tallahassee
New College of Florida, Sarasota
University of Central Florida, Orlando
University of Florida, Gainesville
University of North Florida, Jacksonville
University of South Florida, Tampa
University of West Florida, Pensacola

Picturing Black New Orleans

A Creole Photographer's View
of the Early Twentieth Century

ARTHÉ A. ANTHONY

UNIVERSITY PRESS OF FLORIDA

Gainesville / Tallahassee / Tampa / Boca Raton
Pensacola / Orlando / Miami / Jacksonville / Ft. Myers / Sarasota

Publication of this paperback edition made possible by a Sustaining the Humanities through the American Rescue Plan grant from the National Endowment for the Humanities.

Frontispiece: Florestine Perrault as an adolescent, early 1910s.

Published in the United States of America

First cloth printing, 2012
First paperback printing, 2023

28 27 26 25 24 23   6 5 4 3 2 1

Library of Congress Cataloging-in-Publication Data
Anthony, Arthé A.
Picturing black New Orleans : a Creole photographer's view of the early twentieth century /
Arthé A. Anthony.
p. cm.
Includes bibliographical references and index.
ISBN 978-0-8130-4187-2 (cloth) | ISBN 978-0-8130-8019-2 (pbk.)
1. Collins, Florestine Perrault, 1895–1988. 2. Portrait photographers—United States Biography.
3. African American portrait photographers—Biography. 4. Portrait photography—Louisiana—
New Orleans. 5. African Americans—Louisiana—New Orleans—Portraits. I. Title.
TR140.C64A58 2012
779.'20976335—dc23   2012009803

The University Press of Florida is the scholarly publishing agency for the State University System of Florida, comprising Florida A&M University, Florida Atlantic University, Florida Gulf Coast University, Florida International University, Florida State University, New College of Florida, University of Central Florida, University of Florida, University of North Florida, University of South Florida, and University of West Florida.

University Press of Florida
2046 NE Waldo Road
Suite 2100
Gainesville, FL 32609
http://upress.ufl.edu

In memory of

Jeannette Warburg Altimus and Leslie Anthony Ward

Contents

Illustrations

Too Black to Be White
and Too White to Be Black

To land her first job in Jim Crow New Orleans, she passed for white. As a single, female teenager in the first decade of the twentieth century, she moved out of her parents' home. After a decade of marriage to a jealous iceman whose insecurities were exacerbated by her independence, she got a divorce. Her Creole culture may have circumscribed women's roles, but Florestine Marguerite Perrault—intentionally or not—was often pushing at the edges.

Hers was a world suspended between black and white, too black to be white and too white to be black. Respectable young Creole girls did not leave home unless they were getting married. Once married, fiercely Catholic Creole women stayed married, however dysfunctional the relationship. Divorce was generally out of the question. Proud of their history and traditions as free people of color—*les gens de couleur libre*—and obsessively protective of their mixed racial heritage, Creoles valued appearance as much as reality, if not more so. And Florestine chronicled that culture over nearly three decades as a pioneering black female photographer operating her own New Orleans studio.

In a rabidly racist America where horrific photo postcards of lynchings were peddled as souvenirs, Florestine focused her lenses on the genteel dimensions of black communions and graduations. While a mainstream white culture embraced caricatures of African Americans as sambos, asexual mammies, and pickaninnies, Florestine documented weddings and piano recitals. She photographed the sacred and secular rites of passage that marked special moments in Creole culture. Her photography created a powerful record of middle-class black propriety and dignity, a record providing a glimpse of the rich and varied threads running through the fabric of this vibrant culture.

I use the term "Creole" to define people of color whose ties to New Orleans and southeastern Louisiana begin in the colonial and antebellum periods. Sometimes I use "Creole," "black," and "African American" interchangeably because, despite their white ancestry, Creoles lived on the colored side of the color line.

By going into business for herself, Florestine avoided jobs, such as laundress or seamstress, that were reserved for black women in favor of work that was challenging, lucrative, and offered working conditions she could control. When she opened her studio in 1920, only 101 black women were identified as photographers in the U.S. census, and only Florestine and two white women were listed in the New Orleans city directory as professional photographers. The eldest of six children, Florestine had gone to work in 1909, when she was fourteen, to help support her family. She was hired as a clerk in a Canal Street photo studio only because her complexion was fair enough that whites "couldn't tell whether I was white or colored." Her boss, Jerome Hannafin, gradually expanded her responsibilities and taught her how to make strips of quick-finish—direct positive—pictures. After six years with Hannafin, she worked as a photo finisher with another white photographer, Herbert J. Harvey, on Camp Street.

She later worked in yet another studio on Canal Street where the owner "was so lazy that he would want to go to a show. So he saw that it was to his advantage to teach me how to make pictures so that he could go and leave me in charge, which he did. He saw that I was apt and learned easily. He left me in charge. That is how I began to pick it up, to learn. In fact, he started me doing the finishing part of the work: the developing and the printing. Then finally when he got pushed, he started teaching me how to take pictures." She knew that if the owner or his customers "ever thought I was colored, they probably wouldn't have allowed me to take pictures." Before opening her own studio, she also worked as a stationery embosser and developer for the Eastman Kodak Company—jobs likely to have been contract work requiring her to pass for white to get them.

After she opened her studio in her living room, her work was initially confined to photographing individuals and small groups. She knew many of her subjects in the early stages of her career. Her customers certainly were not all relatives, but photos of relatives are many of the ones that have survived. Two of her favorite subjects were her nieces Germaine and Jean Gardina, her sister Mildred's children. One photo shows Jean holding a teddy bear (photo 1), and Florestine would later make hand-painted photographs of both girls. One hand-painted photograph shows Jean holding a Shirley Temple doll (photo 2). Another photograph is of her sister Germaine with hand-painted fingernails (plate 1). She also photographed them as teenagers probably dressed for a recital in the mid-1940s (plate 2). She later made a picture of Lydia Sindos, the daughter of a family friend, as a junior bridesmaid for a 1945 wedding (plate 3). The engaging portraits Florestine made in the 1920s include one of a beautiful unidentified young woman wearing pearls and

Photo 1. Jean Gardina, Florestine's niece, with teddy bear, early 1930s.

Photo 2. Jean Gardina, Florestine's niece, holding a Shirley Temple doll, mid-1930s.

Photo 3. Unidentified young woman, Bertrand's Studio, early 1920s. Emile LaBranche Jr. Papers. By permission of Amistad Research Center at Tulane University.

Photo 4. Unidentified woman, mid-1920s. The Historic New Orleans Collection, accession no. 2001.79.9.

a headband (photo 3). Another is of an older woman who also wears pearls and a barrette (photo 4).

Florestine was my maternal great-aunt. She operated studios under three names in several locations, first as Bertrand's, then as Claiborne, and finally as Collins. The name changes roughly paralleled her own as she went from Perrault to Bertrand after her first marriage and to Collins after her second. She did not think of herself as an artist, although she clearly was. For her, the studios she owned were businesses. But they were businesses that could give life to fantasies, projecting images of a reality that often could only be dreamed. Her portrait of her friend Mae Fuller, for instance, shows Mae perched seductively on a bench, looking directly at the camera and dressed in the style of a flapper from the Roaring Twenties (photo 5). Mae, in fact, worked as a maid for a dentist during the day and most likely wore a uniform at work.

Photo 5. Mae Fuller in the Roaring Twenties, mid-1920s.

After she retired in 1949, Florestine moved to Los Angeles, where some of her lifelong friends had settled. Although she had stopped working professionally, she continued to make pictures of our family and friends, especially in the 1950s and early 1960s. Although her portraits were treasured family keepsakes, I had taken them for granted. It took more than twenty years before I came to appreciate her story as a photographer and entrepreneur and to understand the significance of the rich visual history she left behind. Almost by accident, I learned bits and pieces of her life when I interviewed her in the mid-1970s while writing my Ph.D. dissertation on Creole history and identity in New Orleans. She was confused by many of my questions because, even then, I thought she had learned photography from her brother Arthur, my grandfather. She corrected that mistaken assumption in no uncertain terms, making it clear that she, the oldest, had introduced her younger siblings to photography.

I was in New Orleans in 2005, four months before Hurricane Katrina, working with curator Ellen Fleurov at Tulane University's Amistad Research Center in search of photographs by Florestine and her male contemporaries for the exhibit *Pictures from Home: Six African American Studio Portrait Photographers in the South, 1900 to 1950.* Our pursuit inadvertently saved several of Florestine's photographs from destruction because relatives had sent them to me. The vast majority that remained in New Orleans homes during the storm either ended up as flotsam in the Gulf of Mexico or were ruined by the rains and flooding. Additional photographs are in family albums of those who left New Orleans and moved to Los Angeles and elsewhere more than fifty years ago. Florestine did not leave business records, diaries, or correspondence.

Only her photographs.

"We Got the Hang of It"

Businesses catering to African Americans were clustered on and near New Orleans's South Rampart Street: department stores, movie theaters, restaurants, hotels, nightclubs, barbershops, dance halls. Train, bus, and streetcar lines boarded and disgorged their passengers at terminals there. Transportation, entertainment, and shopping along South Rampart generated a tide of pedestrian traffic even in the midst of the Great Depression. Florestine, a confident and experienced businesswoman by the mid-1930s, decided to move her studio there, a decision that proved extremely lucrative. Her earlier studios had been downtown, near concentrations of Creoles, near a network of friends and relatives. Now she was taking her business to midtown, to the heart of the African American commercial district, and expanding her customer base to black people from all walks of life.

For as little as ten cents, a walk-in customer could buy a strip of direct positive, or "quick-finish," photographs. The process, most familiar from the once-common coin-operated photo booths in arcades and retail stores, makes an instant picture by imprinting the image directly on the paper. Florestine's first boss had taught her the process, and she and her brother Arthur resolved, "If he can do it, we can do it." "It was nothing but a little box," she said. Arthur and their father, Theophile, built the box to house the machine that cranked out pictures.

That machine was the source of many headaches early on. "When I think of the trouble that thing gave us," she said. "We'd have customers sitting down there waiting, and the darn machine would break down." She knew only one person who could repair it. "We'd have to take the machine out, take the film out, and put the film in a box and go over to this man's house and have him work on the machine," she said. "The customers seemed to not mind; they'd wait until we came back."

Photo 6. Thelma
Perrault Lombard,
Florestine's sister,
mid-1930s.

Despite those initial problems with the quick-finish camera, her new venture "did very well from the very beginning." The studio had a lot of losses, she said, due to mistakes with new equipment and advanced photographic techniques. "We had to learn by trial and error," she said. "We lost a lot of stock on account of trying things out. Pictures would come out bad, and we'd have to make them over. But after a while, we got the hang of it." The studio's hand-painting of direct positive photos is illustrated in a shot of her younger sister Thelma (photo 6).

Florestine "got the hang of it," indeed. Collins Studio thrived during the hard times of the Great Depression. She managed to prosper while the small number of black women working as professional photographers in the country dwindled from 101 in 1920 to only 85 in 1930.[1] She had a loyal customer base, experience and expertise, an excellent location, and cheap direct positive pictures. With more than one-third of black New Orleanians on relief in 1930, and many others working for reduced wages, the range of prices and products she offered was crucial to her studio's success. And her relatively well-to-do customers who could afford the more expensive portraits continued to be a mainstay of her business. Her first year on South Rampart was so successful that she celebrated with a dance only for her customers at the Golden Dragon, a popular nightclub, featuring Joe Robichaux's Orchestra and two floor shows.

Like the majority of black photographers, Florestine worked exclusively for black clients. Racist caricatures of African Americans were persistent and pervasive in mainstream movies and publications, and on billboards and labels for household products from Aunt Jemima Pancake Mix to Gold Dust Twins cleansers. Given those distorted images, black photographers understood that their customers wanted to be represented at their very best. By recognizing and responding to this need, Florestine prospered enough to buy a new two-story home with a large yard on North Galvez Street, where she often hosted large family dinners. She also liked to update her cars and drove to Detroit once with her husband and friends to buy a new Chrysler. As her financial success continued, she built a spacious two-story vacation home, Shangri-La, on Haynes Boulevard, within walking distance of segregated Lincoln Beach. One of her nieces, Carmelita Perrault Lagarde, remembers the home's gazebo and picnic grounds that Florestine frequently rented out. Ever the entrepreneur, she also rented out a very small apartment behind her house.

The Depression created a heightened sense of political urgency in black communities across the country, and many organizations and individuals in New Orleans intensified their struggle for civil rights and racial betterment. The fight to gain voting rights and end employment discrimination clearly had an impact on Florestine's world as she and her second husband, Herbert Collins, became engaged in community and civic life. In the mid-1930s, they joined Central Congregational Church, known for being a hub of social and political activities. As central as Catholicism is to Creole culture, Florestine was not allowed to remain in the Catholic Church after her divorce. She and her husband also became members of the local branch of the National Association for the Advancement of Colored People. She launched her own holiday charity with a Christmas party in her studio for poor children, featuring gifts and two Santa Clauses. A photo of her 1939 party made its way into the pages of the *Louisiana Weekly*, a black newspaper.[2] She was listed as one of four New Orleans photographers in a 1940 journal promoting black businesses.

Debates about racism rippled daily through Florestine's community. Just as important were discussions of the importance of black entrepreneurs and the need for Negro consumers to patronize them as part of a solution to the economics of Jim Crow. The *Louisiana Weekly* published a host of articles on the national efforts to combat segregation and the international struggle against colonialism and imperialism in the Caribbean and sub-Saharan Africa. The newspaper also encouraged its readers to write about "Race Advancement and Community Progress" in one of its open forums.[3]

After she relocated and expanded, Florestine brought relatives into her business. Collins Studio enhanced the Perrault family's local reputation and provided an economic underpinning for several of her siblings and their families.

Photo 7. Theophile Perrault, Collins's father, mid-1940s.

Florestine's sister Thelma Lombard was a saleswoman. Her sister Mildred Gardina and a family friend, Walterine Celestine, were co-managers. Her brother Arthur opened his own photography studios—first in Atlanta and later in New Orleans—only after learning photographic skills from his sister. Their father, who was in his early sixties in the mid-1930s, also took on tasks at the studio and was photographed as a dashing older man wearing a long coat and hat and holding a cigarette (photo 7). Her mother, as her grandmother had done, oversaw

Photo 8. Marie Louise Pierce, at her graduation from Valena C. Jones Normal School, 1935. By permission of Jari Honora.

household responsibilities such as cooking dinner since Florestine worked long hours. Her studio was open seven days a week except during the summer.

As Florestine's customer base expanded after her move to South Rampart, so did her social network. Her circle of friends now included black people with dark complexions, as her second husband had, and others from "uptown." Color prejudice would have routinely excluded these darker-complexioned people from associating with the often clannish Creoles. Most black and white working-class Louisianans were mired in poverty in the late 1920s and 1930s. Scholars have noted the popularity of photography during the Great Depression, noting that many could not resist owning and looking at photographs. In New Orleans, most African Americans—who were already poor before the Depression—had to make great sacrifices in the 1930s.

Photo 9. Henry C. Sindos, officer of the Standard Life Insurance Company, early 1940s. Lydia Sindos Adams Papers. By permission of Amistad Research Center at Tulane University.

Although stretched thin by poverty and extraordinarily high black unemployment, the basic fabric of black family and institutional life for the elite in New Orleans did not completely unravel. Baptisms, weddings, First Communions, and graduations were important parts of Florestine's business. She captured moments such as Marie Louise Pierce's graduation from Valena C. Jones Normal School in 1935 (photo 8). It was "a big thing," said my mother, Arthé Perrault Anthony, who is also Florestine's niece. People "wanted to preserve their heritage, or they wanted to document events in their lives," she said. The symbolic meaning of family photographs was widely understood and included even poor black sharecroppers in the South who often owned "colored photographs of themselves."[4]

The social status of many of Florestine's elite customers and friends is difficult to understand from a contemporary perspective because many of them worked jobs that would not be considered elite today. Some of the women were cigar makers, seamstresses, hairdressers, homemakers, and school teachers. Men's jobs ran the gamut from craftsmen to porters to laborers and included doctors, entrepreneurs, and businessmen, such as Henry C. Sindos, a founding officer of the Standard Life Insurance Company of Louisiana and former grocer. He was dressed formally for his portrait with a hat, tie, and pin-striped suit (photo 9). Sindos's company echoed a New Orleans Creole business tradition with roots in the late eighteenth century. Creoles did not enjoy full citizenship, but as free people of color they did have social and economic privileges—freedom of movement, exemption from curfew, owning banks and property, including slaves. But those days began coming to an end in the two decades before the Civil War as a terrified white population prepared to do battle with winds of change blowing in from the North.

3

"The Moment You're a Creole, It Was la Même Chose"

As the Civil War approached, Louisiana's whites, by then a minority of the population, feared that Creoles would join forces with rebellious slaves. Newly imposed restrictions meant that Creoles could no longer freely assemble, and their word that they were free did not suffice. They had to carry papers proving it. Slaves had a 9:00 p.m. curfew that was expanded to apply to Creoles. As many researchers have noted, some fled the state for Haiti, Cuba, or Mexico in an effort to escape the swelling racist tide.

Creole status had declined drastically from the Spanish Period between 1769 and 1803, when their population had risen to one-third of African Americans in New Orleans. Following Britain's victory in the Seven Years' War—known in North America as the French and Indian War—France transferred Louisiana to Spain, its ally against the English. When Napoleon needed money to finance his military adventures in Europe, he demanded the territory back from Spain and sold it—Thomas Jefferson's Louisiana Purchase—to the United States in 1803.

In the forty years under the Spanish, clear paths to freedom were codified for slaves, who could initiate the purchase of their own liberty, at times whether their masters agreed to the sale or not, under a process known as *coartación*. Still, free people of color occupied an uncertain middle ground in New Orleans's economic and cultural caste system, with whites on top and black slaves below. Many free people of color owned businesses, banks, real estate, and slaves. Some free men "were highly educated, cultured, and cosmopolitan" and looked down on slaves.[1]

The racial mixture among Creoles was, for the most part, French, Spanish, and African. No level of sophistication, however, protected them from the indignities all blacks suffered in the decade before the Civil War if not earlier. Generally the kinds of jobs free blacks had were unrestricted in New Orleans. This, too, changed. Their economic status began to be challenged in the mid-1840s by the influx of white immigrants from other states, and ordinances were increasingly imposed to circumscribe many aspects of black life. One law prevented any assembly of colored people, slave or free. It became illegal for them to play cards or dominoes, or for free people of color to have balls with slaves.

By the time Florestine was born in 1895, whatever privileges or wealth New Orleans's free people of color might have enjoyed before the Civil War had long since been buried beneath an avalanche of Jim Crow laws and customs. Her relatives, though, had been among the substantial number of Creoles who owned property in the racially mixed Faubourg Tremé neighborhood, where white and black families lived side by side in the early nineteenth century.

The first child of Theophile Perrault and Emilie Jules, Florestine was named after one of her father's older cousins (photo 10). Shortly after she opened her studio

Photo 10. Florestine Marguerite Perrault as an adolescent, early 1910s.

Photo 11. Emilie Jules Perrault, Florestine's mother, early 1920s.

in 1920, she made a photograph of her mother, an attractive, elegant woman captured in a pensive pose (photo 11). Florestine can trace her paternal lineage to Michel Guillaume Perrault, a white man born in Quebec to French immigrant parents in 1726. He settled in New Orleans in the mid-1770s after stops in France and Martinique. He never married, but he fathered a son, Firmin, with Françoise Lalande, Florestine's great-great-grandmother, a free woman of color. Françoise was about nineteen when she gave birth to Firmin in September 1786. Her relationship with Michel—who was forty years her senior—lasted about six years, and Firmin appears to be Michel's only child.

Perrault served in Louisiana's Spanish Militia, fighting against the British in the American War of Independence. He and his white extended family ascended New Orleans's social ladder as they prospered well enough for him to buy a plantation on the city's Tchoupitoulas Coast along the Mississippi River. Just before his death in 1790, Michel sold Françoise a house next door to his own home in the French Quarter. His provisions for his colored family included giving Françoise "1500 pesos for her 'infinite services,'" and their four-year-old-son, Firmin, was given the use of a slave.[2] Michel's name does not appear on Firmin's baptismal certificate, but there is no evidence that he ever denied paternity. Firmin went by the last name of Perrault all his life and is mentioned in both of Michel's wills. In addition, one of Michel's nieces was Firmin's godmother. "Often the whites who served as godparents were related to their racially mixed godchildren," notes historian Virginia Meacham Gould.[3]

Louisiana genealogist Gregory Osborn conjectures that based on Françoise's last name, Lalande, and other historical records, her mother most likely was Marguerite, a former slave on the white Lalande Dapremont plantation adjacent to Michel Perrault's property. Mixed-race children during this period were invariably the offspring of black mothers and white fathers. Although some members of the Perrault family could afford to buy property and build homes in the middle of the nineteenth century, they were not as wealthy as a number of their colored Tremé neighbors who owned plantations or were real estate developers before the Civil War. Firmin's son Appollinaire was well enough off to buy properties for $4,650 in 1852, and $1,200 in 1859, a combined sum of more than $155,000 in today's dollars. A photograph of a cottage he built on the land is included in an architectural inventory compiled by Roulhac Toledano and Mary Louise Christovich.[4]

Creole men fought in the War of 1812 and were members of the Louisiana Native Guards during the Civil War. The Native Guards were first organized as a unit in the Confederate army but were disbanded when whites decided that arming people of color might not be such a good idea. They were later reorganized as a unit in the Union army, but scholars disagree on how many of the former

Photo 12. Oscar Perrault, Florestine's grandfather, late 1880s.

Confederate guardsmen made the transition. Firmin, Florestine's great-grand-father, and other members of the Perrault family served in the First Battalion of Free Men of Color in the 1814 Battle of New Orleans. During the Civil War, Florestine's grandfather, Oscar Perrault (1829–1905), was a private in the Seventy-Third, Seventy-Fourth, and Ninety-First Regiments of the United States Colored Troops. He was photographed in his later years dressed as a stately gentleman (photo 12).

Despite the relative decline of their special privileges by the late nineteenth century, the majority of Creoles in New Orleans continued to see themselves as a culturally distinct group. And in many respects they were, given their Catholicism, French-language traditions, geographical concentration in downtown wards, occupational patterns, and their sense of history as descendants of free people of color. Many saw themselves as ethnically separate from other African Americans, insisting that Creole was not black. Creoles in New Orleans had a social cohesiveness and many generations of urban living, unlike what they saw as the unsophisticated overwhelming majority of African Americans, who were rural agricultural workers or relatively recent arrivals to southern cities.

Creoles refused to be classified with the publicly maligned freedmen and their descendants. Underlying this perception—a view that was carried over into the twentieth century—was a refusal to submit to the dichotomy explicit in segregation: that all Caucasians were superior and all Negroes were inferior. Rather than accept this view, Creoles created a middle ground for themselves; even though they were not legally granted the rights afforded whites, by no means would they tolerate categorization with blacks.

Creoles sought—and to a certain extent found—if not protection at least comfort in their own world because they were able to exercise a degree of control over it. By avoiding extensive contact with African Americans, they were able to separate themselves—at least psychologically—from other blacks, thereby reaffirming in their own minds that they were different from them. Given this thrust to establish a separate and superior identity from other African Americans, it is not surprising that Perrault men married Creole women of similar backgrounds, including immigrants from Haiti and Cuba. Florestine's paternal grandmother was a free woman of color from Louisiana whose Cuban-born husband, François, was a carpenter. His family most likely immigrated to New Orleans from Cuba after having left Haiti with refugees who supported the losing side in the Haitian Revolution. They landed in Cuba but were expelled in 1809 after Napoleon invaded Spain, Cuba's mother country.

By the early decades of the twentieth century, older Creoles such as Florestine's grandparents would certainly have identified strongly with what had become a relatively homogeneous colored Creole culture. For the vast majority of Florestine's generation, the group's Caribbean or Mexican pasts were only vague memories. Any distinction between people of Haitian descent and other Creoles disappeared. "The moment you're a Creole, it was *la même chose*," said Gaston F. Moore Sr. (1890–1981), one of Florestine's contemporaries. When Florestine was born, the melding of these cultures had already taken place almost a century earlier.

"We Couldn't Sit in the Front"

Florestine dropped out of school to go to work after completing the sixth grade in 1909. Still, her education was one grade higher than New Orleans provided black youngsters. In 1900, the Orleans Parish school board eliminated all public school grades for colored students beyond the fifth, making it all but impossible for the vast majority of these students to attend secondary school.[1] The board did not open a secondary school for black students until 1917, when what came to be called "McDonogh 35" was created. Many Creole students of Florestine's generation were educated at a combination of parochial and public schools, depending on family income and the proximity of classrooms. Florestine, for example, attended two small private schools offered in the teachers' homes before enrolling in the Daniel Hand Preparatory School run by the American Missionary Association's Straight University.

The Protestant Congregationalist Church established Straight, a school highly respected for the quality of its education, its mission of service to the community, and the major leadership roles blacks played in the institution. It was located near Creole neighborhoods, and, more important, it did not aggressively attempt to proselytize students, unlike some other Protestant schools. Florestine's father had been enrolled in the same school in 1908 while his daughter was still a student there.

Creoles had long taken pride in their literacy, and before the Civil War, New Orleans's free black community "probably had a literacy level which exceeded that of the white population of the state as a whole," Donald E. DeVore and Joseph Logsdon write.[2] Regardless of how tight money was, Creoles generally were not enthusiastic about sending their children to public schools. Many parents felt the public school curriculum was superficial and the schools overcrowded. Some Creoles, however, rejected public schools simply because they were open—at least theoretically—to the black public. In this period, most Creoles looked down on darker-skinned African Americans and would not allow their children to attend school with other black children.

One option was Catholic religious instruction, especially for younger children. Florestine attended a small school run by her godmother. "That's when I got my basics," she said. This school conducted in her godmother's home was only for light-skinned Creole children. Since her godmother was known as a *passant blanc,* someone passing for white, "the darker class of people would never attempt to get into a place like that because they knew her for what she was," she said. "I'm sure there weren't any dark children in the classes at the time because I know my godmother wouldn't have had them. I don't remember seeing them. But knowing her, and knowing what she was trying to be, she wouldn't have had any dark children. Even if it was the children of people that she knew, she still wouldn't have them."

Florestine also attended another small Catholic school where the teacher, Anna Meyers, taught children "how to make their First Communion," she said. "After they made their First Communion, she let them go; she taught them Catholicism, in other words."[3] Meyers was principal of the Guardian Angels School for Colored Boys and Girls, which she housed in her home on North Prieur Street in downtown New Orleans from 1899 to 1909. Attending private schools such as those that Florestine describes was commonplace for members of her generation. Judith Fluger Meteye (1903–1989) went to "Miss Angelina's school," where she received her limited education. "That's the only school that I ever went to. I never went to a public school." My paternal great-aunt Alice Simon Chevalier (1905–1981) said her school, run by "Miss Stephanie[,] . . . had hundreds of children that she used to teach catechism" in her home. Alice's husband, Everett Chevalier (1900–1980), also remembered going to Miss Stephanie's school before enrolling in the public Bienville School, adding that Miss Stephanie charged "ten cents a week for catechism and teaching" and an introduction to reading and writing. Much like Florestine's godmother and Meyers, she converted rooms in their homes into classrooms to provide catechism instruction and a rudimentary education for Creole pupils.

By enrolling their children in these private schools, parents were circumventing racial segregation and Protestantism. No matter how limited these schools were, they played an important role in the Creole community's self-image of its exclusivity because these parents were sending their children to private schools that charged tuition. Enola Cavanaugh (1893–1980), one of Florestine's contemporaries, remembered her father "couldn't see that you should go somewhere where it was free; you had to pay that dollar a month." At the same time, the women who ran most of these small schools were conforming to the Creole community's very conventional view that women should not work outside the home.

Although Creole parents wanted their children's formal education to be complemented by religious instruction, most parents did not directly challenge the church's racism, nor did they expect their children to do so. Florestine remembered Meyers, her Catholic school teacher, marching her children to church every day for Mass. When the children entered, they would be seated in the rear pews. "We couldn't sit in the front," she said. Some parents strongly resented the church's racism, but instead of challenging it, one father preferred that his son pass for white while preparing for his confirmation rather than be segregated in his local parish church, which is why he made his confirmation at St. Louis Cathedral.

Catholic children had two communions—the "little communion," when they were seven and the "big communion," or confirmation, when they were twelve. "We were taught that once you were seven years old you were responsible for your sins," said Alice Simon Chevalier. "When you made your 'big' communion you had to be dressed up with an umbrella and everything. You had your prayer book and your beads wrapped around your left hand, and you had an umbrella." Girls had white umbrellas, white gloves, and white shoes. "Then your mama would walk you to death going from one friend's house to another," she said. "And you had what they called a satchel hanging on your arm. And everywhere that you would go, they would give you a nickel or a dime—you'd make a collection."

Her husband, Everett, described similarly elegant attire for boys—a white suit, white shirt, and white tie as well as a long decorated candle along with a rosary and missal. Early in her career, Florestine photographed a young man formally dressed in white for his "big" communion, wearing white gloves and holding his missal and rosary beads in his right hand and carrying a decorated candle in his left. He stands next to a seated woman, beautifully dressed in white and holding a diploma (photo 13).

Confirmation had lifelong importance for Alice Chevalier, who at age seventy-two still had her confirmation dress, and her seventy-seven-year-old husband had his prayer book from that special day. Florestine kept a beautiful portrait of herself taken on her confirmation day in 1906, when she was eleven years old. Although the bottom half of the photograph is missing, it shows that her dress and veil were clearly made with great care. Both would have been handmade as was most likely true of her parasol and satchel. She also carries an elaborately decorated candle and holds a fan. Only part of her parasol, a ceremonial accessory, can be seen (photo 14).

Catholic devotion to Mary was also integrated into Creole life as evinced by children and adults wearing a "scapular, two small pieces of brown wool cloth worn over the shoulders as a symbolic undergarment."[4] In addition, children frequently belonged to the Children of Mary, as did Florestine's younger friend

Photo 13. Unidentified graduate and communicant, early 1920s. The Historic New Orleans Collection, accession no. 2001.79.7.

Photo 14. Florestine Perrault, "big" communion, 1906.

Jeannette Warburg (1905–2003). She remembers participating in the Children of Mary first as an "angel of Mary," then becoming a "child of Mary" after she made her First Communion.

All Saints' Day on November 1 was another of the many religious traditions Catholics observed. Families visited cemeteries to clean their relatives' tombs and pay respects to the dead. "On All Saints' Day we would always go to the graveyard well-dressed with a nice fall outfit, whether it was hot or cold," recalled Eva Jamet Prevost, fifteen years Florestine's junior. "When you came into the house, the mothers always made cake or they had some punch, or they'd have something to give you as you passed each of your friends' houses."

5

"She Never Went Outside One Day to Work"

Whether they were the descendants of ex-slaves or of free people of color, black people in New Orleans endured very hard times at the turn of the twentieth century. Mothers, wives, and daughters had to work just to keep their families afloat. Florestine's father earned decent wages as a bricklayer, but his work was seasonal because of frequent, heavy rains. Florestine helped with her salary from the photo studio. But when a father died, leaving a widow with several children, his family was often reduced to grinding poverty.

Alice Chevalier was three years old when her father died, leaving her mother, Anecia Paltron Simon, forty-seven, a widow with seven children. Anecia did her best to support her children by sewing piecework. But everyone else in the family went to work as soon as they were able. More than fifty years later, Chevalier and one of her sisters were still very emotional about the devastating impact of their father's death on the family.

Although at fourteen she was legally underage, Chevalier worked in a commercial laundry where she earned three dollars per week. In a 1977 interview, she remembered catching sheets and pillowcases to fold after they came out of the mangle, or pressing machine. Her hours were "for as long as they wanted," she said. As low as her salary was, she would go into a panic when inspectors checking on employees' ages came. "We used to hide in the toilet," she told me.

When Creole girls and women worked outside their homes, they tried to avoid work as servants for whites. Aside from the long hours and poor pay, there was an overarching fear that Creole women would be subjected to sexual harassment and abuse. Eva Prevost said she had an opportunity to sew "for one of the richest white families. But my husband said, no, that the white man would make advances on me and so forth." Despite the reality of sexual harassment, many black women who worked outside of their homes had to take whatever work was available.

And sometimes that work was the sex trade, especially in a city like New Orleans, where prostitution was highly publicized and legal. The city itself was often depicted in literature as a mythical courtesan. The presence of the infamous Storyville red-light district from 1897 to 1917 must have heightened the anxieties of poor black families about their young daughters' abilities to find respectable work.

Women's paid labor was necessary, but many husbands and fathers tried to exercise control over where the women in their families worked. Creole men of Florestine's generation were very emphatic about the types of work that were respectable and the distinction between women working for wages "inside" or "outside" of the home. George McKenna Sr. (1890–1992), who knew Florestine's father well, was adamant that his mother, Elizabeth, never worked outside. He came from a family of twelve, and when work for his father, a cigar maker, was scarce, his mother would sew, he said. She would also make a fried rice pastry called *calas*, and her children would wrap them in a towel to keep them warm and sell them "five for a nickel" on the streets. "She never went outside one day to work," he said. She also made the local candy known as pralines to earn money, and she ran "a little store in the front room," he said.

Fears of working outside were pushed aside when the reality of a family's poverty demanded pragmatic solutions. Manuella Adams Robert (1886–1969), for example, worked as a maid in the Monteleone Hotel in the French Quarter when her husband, Vincent, a mail carrier, died at a young age (photo 15). Only a few women became entrepreneurs, owning beauty parlors, dressmaking and millinery shops, or, in some exceptional cases, running small private schools like the ones Florestine attended.

Just as the occupations varied, so did the working conditions within particular occupations. Ten years older than Florestine, Theresa Holland (1885–1985) remembered working on St. Peter Street in the 1890s as a young girl, sewing kimonos at fifteen cents a dozen in a crude factory. They also had chemises to sew at forty cents a dozen, "but you had to work a little harder" to earn that, she said. "And after you'd get the forty cents, it wasn't yours; you had to bring it home" to give to your mother. Holland's mother had seven children with the white unmarried shoemaker who lived next door, and she did not work for wages outside of the home. Holland's aunts took their niece to learn how to sew "because I had to learn how to do something—I was a girl," she said.

A number of women sewed in their homes, making men's pants from precut bundles. They would get their bundles from shops or factories, and were paid by the piece. Other women, like Eugenie Armant Hubbard, worked in clothing

Photo 15. Manuella Adams Robert, family friend, 1930s.

factories. What was to be a temporary job after her husband fell ill became twenty-seven years of coat making for Hubbard. "After he got better, he didn't want me to work, but I told him that I wasn't going to stop working because I didn't know what would happen," she said. "I'd have to look for another job if something were to come up. So I decided to keep on."

Florestine's contemporary Marceline Bucksell Taylor (1892–1978) was among those seamstresses considered *modistes* because of their superior workmanship. She sewed at home for private customers, a career path her mother dictated by telling her she had to teach or sew. "I preferred sewing because after you married in those days you couldn't teach anymore," she said in a 1977 interview. Taylor sewed exclusively for whites initially, but eventually began sewing for black women. Her customers most likely were exclusively one race or the other because it would have been unacceptable for a white woman to be kept waiting for a fitting while Taylor assisted a colored client.

Once she began sewing exclusively for blacks, perhaps in the mid-1930s, her creations for confirmation, debutante and Mardi Gras balls, weddings, graduations, and music recitals were often photographed by Florestine and other black photographers. My grandfather photographed my mother, Arthé Perrault Anthony, in the elaborate 1947 debutante queen's dress Taylor had made (photo 16).

Taylor began sewing in a white-owned dressmaker's shop where all of the seamstresses were passive Creole girls. She clearly saw herself as different. "When I went there—I had my nerve—I asked for a dollar and a half a day; and that was big money," she said. "Some of them weren't even getting that, and they had been there for years with her."

Much like Florestine, Taylor learned quickly and realized that she could use her growing sewing skills to start her own business. She watched her boss carefully and was soon helping her fit customers. "Really, the woman did think a lot of me, but I was trying to learn the things that she knew because I had figured that someday I was going out for myself." Taylor's private sewing business for rich white customers, including many of her former boss's wealthy clients, grew to such an extent that some neighbors were suspicious about the expensive cars that came to her house, and one reported her to the police, thinking she was running a house of prostitution.

Other women, whose families were also pressed financially, recalled working as children to perform a variety of housekeeping chores for white neighbors. In spite of their low wages, these women did not consider their lives dreadful or filled with drudgery. Judith Meteye told me that although she had to work as a child, her "younger life was very happy, being with friends, and being so close to my family." Her family's poverty was such that she was forced to leave school after the third grade to begin working. Her mother was Creole, and her father

Photo 16. Arthé C. Perrault as debutante, 1947, photographed by Arthur J. Perrault.
By permission of Arthé Perrault Anthony.

a German American who lived with his colored family and "was a wonderful daddy."

Meteye's and Holland's stories illustrate that having a white father did not necessarily protect a family from harsh economic realities. Meteye's father's parents were German immigrants, and he was a member of the New Orleans Police Department, "the worst paid and . . . most overworked of any force among the nation's major cities."[1] As a result of her father's low wages, she was forced to go to work. "I would go out and make little day's work for the people in my neighborhood—the white folks I'm talking about," she said. "When I was about fourteen I went and worked in a factory." Meteye also was underage when she began her first factory job, and her fellow workers would "rush me into the dressing room" when inspectors came. "I was very tall and slender," she said. "They'd rush me in there and put a long skirt [on me]. I'd go back to my machine and I'd pass as if I was of age. I worked that way a good while."

6

"I Tore Out Barefooted,
Running down to the Track"

When she was eighty, Florestine described with great fondness her childhood home as half of a double house her family rented from a relative who had built it. "It was a nice house," she said. "The street was a mud street; a cow used to pass in front" every day. That street became the reason she offered for moving out of her parents' home when she was still single. The move, she said, was to avoid having to be carried across the frequently muddy street to keep her skirts clean.

It was a plausible enough story if not subjected to scrutiny. New Orleans's streets were muddy all over town in the early twentieth century, filled with "the omnipresent stench of animal carcasses, full privy vaults, and stagnant ditches" due to inadequate drainage and sewage systems.[1] So the problem of keeping her skirts clean would have followed her wherever she moved. She actually left home because her father accused her of "borrowing" without permission money he kept at home for his Masonic lodge. But she needed a cover story lest her name be dragged through more mud than her skirts.

However squalid the streets may have been, Creoles of that generation remember their neighborhoods as vibrant, with peddlers selling fruits, vegetables, oysters, and shrimps from horse-drawn wagons. Youngsters fished from the old basin on Claiborne and Lafitte and could get crabs outside their front door. As much fun as they were having, they were also putting food on their families' tables. Adults collected blackberries and Spanish moss—a common mattress stuffing—to sell on the city streets, or went to Lake Pontchartrain to catch soft-shell crabs to sell three for a dime.

To complicate matters in the Perrault household after Florestine moved out, her father also left home and moved in with another woman. But he continued to support his family and remained involved in their lives, so much so that his grandchildren years later were unaware that their grandparents had ever separated. The name of the woman he moved in with and the length of time he was there have long been forgotten. The importance of maintaining the air of respectability made that separation a taboo topic—a memory that has been erased from the Perrault family history. Any hard feelings between Florestine and her father over the missing money must have been quickly resolved. They maintained a close bond throughout his life until he died in the mid-1950s in her home in Los Angeles.

After she left home, Florestine boarded with Louisa Czarnowski Fuller (1872–1943), the widowed mother of eight children and the grandmother of Walter and Andrew Young, the former ambassador to the United Nations and mayor of

Photo 17. Louisa Czarnowski Fuller, the mother of Daisy Fuller Young and Mae Fuller Keller, late 1930s.

Atlanta. Three of Mrs. Fuller's children—Mae, Daisy, and Walter—were Florestine's close friends. She would later photograph Mrs. Fuller sitting in an armchair,
looking very much like the matriarch she was (photo 17). Before she moved in
with the Fullers, Florestine was already romantically involved with Walter (1895–
1975), the youngest son, who was living with his family and working as an elevator
tender. But her jealousy over him seeing another woman, and his suspicion that
she was involved with a white photographer, ended that romance. Florestine then
began dating Eilert Bertrand (1889–1947), who would soon become her husband.

Her marriage came after she had moved to Biloxi, Mississippi, to recuperate
from surgery, but details of the operation are unclear. She boarded with Mabel
Angle Warburg, whose husband, Joseph Daniel Warburg, a highly skilled stone-
cutter, had been forced into retirement by illness. He and his wife had left New
Orleans and resettled in Biloxi in 1910. Biloxi, with its annual influx of wealthy
whites from the frozen East and North, was a great location for a boardinghouse.
"Those rich people would bring their chauffeurs with them," Jeannette recalled.
The black employees sought accommodations in the Negro part of town because
they were barred from white hotels and could not have afforded them even if Jim
Crow restrictions had not existed. Boardinghouses such as Mabel's were essential
for black travelers all over the country and were later compiled in guides such as
the *Green Book for African Americans*.

The Warburgs' household was lively with the presence of boarders, a young
niece and nephew, Jeannette and her brother Alex. The niece and nephew had
joined their aunt when their parents' interracial relationship dissolved, leaving
their mother, Emma, with six children. Emma was forced to fend for herself, the
reason why she and several of her children passed for white. Jeannette enjoyed
living with her aunt, uncle, and brother, and took the Warburgs' last name as her
own. Florestine made a picture of Jeannette's brother Alex in the early 1920s at her
New Orleans studio (photo 18). Biloxi did not provide many amusements for its
colored citizens with the exception of an ice cream parlor, visits to the seashore—
on the day it was open to blacks—and socializing in one another's homes. The
biggest excitement was to go to the train station on Sundays. It "was a big event on
a Sunday evening," Jeannette remembered, "just taking a walk down to the railroad
station to see the people getting off the train and those who were going back to
New Orleans."

In the summer of 1917, one midweek visit to the train station was especially
memorable because Florestine was coming to town. "When I heard the train
whistle, I had on my little dress, and I tore out barefooted, running down to the
track," Jeannette Warburg Altimus recalled. It was virtually love at first sight and
the start of what turned out to be seventy years of friendship. At seventy-two years
of age nearly six decades later, Altimus recalled that Florestine was expecting to

Photo 18. Alex Moses,
Jeannette Warburg's
brother, early 1920s.

meet someone much older. "I was twelve years old, and she said that is why she took such a liking to me because she thought I was the cutest thing and so small. And I said I took a liking to you because you gave me a banana."

Jeannette left Biloxi after she turned sixteen four years later because the local public high school for blacks did not offer classes beyond the tenth grade. She moved to New Orleans and enrolled at Xavier Preparatory, a private Catholic school. But she could no longer afford the tuition after her father died during

Photo 19. Florestine Perrault Bertrand, self-portrait, early 1920s.

her senior year. She then entered Guillaume's commercial school, the only secretarial school available for young colored girls in New Orleans, and moved in with Florestine and Eilert. At this point, the couple had been married for five years, and Florestine offered Jeannette free room and board.

Florestine had married Eilert Bertrand, who was seven years her senior, in a civil ceremony in the fall of 1917. But the independent-minded Florestine probably had not imagined a relationship that was as stifling as this marriage turned out to be. In the late 1910s, Bertrand worked as a delivery man for the Pelican Ice Company, driving a horse and wagon on a route that included Mrs. Fuller's house on North Prieur Street, where Florestine lived. He may have met Florestine there. However they met, his attraction to her is easy to imagine, given her beauty and reserve as her self-portrait illustrates (photo 19). She didn't drink or dance, and "she was a different class of woman than what Bertrand was used to," Jeannette said, suggesting that Florestine was not as loose as other women Bertrand knew.

Florestine's friends never quite understood her interest in Bertrand, other than to get back at Walter Fuller. Bertrand was not a particularly handsome man. In fact, Altimus recalls being quite disappointed by his appearance when she first met him because he had lost an eye in an accident. (To this day, my father jokingly refers to him as "Bertrand, the one-eyed iceman.") It is clear that by the summer of 1917, Florestine and Bertrand had come to an understanding about their relationship because he paid Mrs. Warburg four dollars per week for Florestine's room and board in Biloxi.

When she was married to Bertrand, she said she had to "walk the chalk line" because he was "one of the most jealous men on earth." Her socializing was limited to occasionally going to the Pythian Temple Roof Garden dances on Saturday nights, but never going out to events like the Mardi Gras balls that were the highlight of each year's social season. Bertrand, from all accounts, was a conventional man who was fearful—perhaps with good reason—of losing his extraordinarily attractive wife had she been able to socialize as she pleased.

"We Never Bothered about Sex"

Intraracial color prejudice, conservative Catholic morality, and anxiety about white male sexual exploitation created a tension between Creole children and their parents around dating. In the early decades of the twentieth century, the Creole community's prejudice against most dark-skinned Negroes was intense. Marguerite "Mag" Montegut Perez (1902–2000), a feisty close friend of Florestine, and her older sister, Bertha Montegut Tate (1905–1990), said their mother often reacted violently when they violated her color code. "We couldn't have any dark boyfriends," Perez said. Older relatives also strictly forbade dark-skinned beaus, "but I didn't pay them no mind," she said. "That's one thing about me."

She named several "dark—not dark—black" male friends with whom she would go to dances on the Pythian Temple's Roof Garden. "I think those boys were the best dancers," she said. Moreover, she explained, "they were more sensible than our Creole boys." Her older sister agreed. For her daring, Perez was often severely punished, as Tate sadly recalled: "They'd knock her down, or slap her down." But both sisters were proud of Perez's defiance, noting that her "dark boyfriends were different." Creole boys "thought they were just too much," Tate said. Such defiance, while not widespread, was not altogether unusual. Florestine and her friend Perez had much in common in terms of their strong-willed determination to break through many of the social conventions and restrictions of their day.

If color prejudice were not enough, some young Creole women of Florestine's generation also chafed under other restrictions their parents and the church imposed. One young woman thought kissing a boy was a mortal sin. "I often talk to my sister about that," said Yvonne Johnson Labat (1904–1983). "We never bothered about sex with boys while we were having fun, laughing, dancing. I don't remember that any of us worried about sex like the young people do today."

Courtship was limited to sitting on a sofa and "talking, talking, talking," she said. "Once you were going to get married, maybe there would be a little petting." When young men visited young women, "routinely her little sister or somebody sat right next to you," Andrew Young Sr. recalled. "And you'd have to go to the show chaperoned," said Young, who graduated from Howard University's dental school in 1921.

Young people could meet at one of the dances held at churches or sponsored by benevolent societies. A group of young women would organize a dance, hire a band, rent the hall, and serve refreshments—lemonade or punch and sandwiches. Admission ranged from fifteen cents to a quarter, and invitations "were only given to those that were in your own circle; no one else was invited," Florestine's neighbor Lydia Gumbel Sindos said. "They'd dance until about twelve or one o'clock" under the supervision of chaperones. "Every girl had a chaperone," she said. "They had two long benches that was chaperones' row."

Alice Chevalier remembered that she and her sisters could walk to and from these "very nice affairs." They seldom had car fare, she said. "And you danced half of the night on a cup of punch, or an orange, or something like that. Your mama would be there with you. I couldn't go out without my mama like the young girls of today. She had to be with me. When you finished dancing, the man would treat you to a cup of punch, or an orange. There was no liquor. We had a good time."

One woman who asked not to be identified recalled that when she turned nineteen, she imagined only one way of escaping from her parents' clutches: "Lord, Jesus, I'm going to marry," she resolved, "because this is too strict. I didn't care if I stayed with the man two or three days—I was going to marry." And for all the power the Catholic Church held over Creoles, some young women, unlike Labat, did "bother about sex" and had children out of wedlock, disregarding the church's admonition that doing so was "a sacrilege and mortal sin," as Eva Prevost explained.

Yet some couples who did marry were afraid to tell their parents, even when the parents approved of the groom. Sindos and her husband married in 1927, but they both went to their respective homes after the wedding. "About a week later, I told my mother, and she was very much outdone," Sindos said. A judge had married them, but they could not move in together until they had the marriage blessed. Even then, they did not immediately move in together. Marguerite Perez and her husband, Wilbur, waited six months to tell her mother about their marriage. "We didn't know how to tell her," Perez said. "People had been telling her that we were married. When I did make up my mind to tell her, she didn't want to hear it. She was mad about it. She liked Wilbur; I don't know why we were married secretly."

Sexuality was not a topic women of Florestine's generation discussed openly or easily. After Florestine died, a 1908 edition of pioneering sex researcher Havelock Ellis's *Studies in the Psychology of Sex* was found among her personal effects. One historian described Ellis's work as appealing to "elite, radical [white] women" in the 1910s.[1] Since Florestine does not fully fit that description, Ellis's book obviously had a broader appeal. Literate men and women with a curiosity about sex would have been drawn to its pages. Ellis made influential contributions to the growing field of sexology, which acknowledged the importance of women's sexuality and marital sexual fulfillment.

Unlike many African American women who moved to northeastern and midwestern cities during the Great Migration that started during World War I, most Creole young women chose to fight their battles at home rather than leave in search of better-paying jobs and greater freedom from racial oppression. Young Creole women—and to a lesser extent young men—stuck close to home because of their strong family ties and already available jobs. In addition, generations of families such as Florestine's had lived in the largest city in the South, making the lure of an urban life away from home not as appealing as it was for rural southern migrants. Of course, some Creole families moved to New Orleans from small towns in southern Louisiana such as Opelousas, New Roads, and St. Martinville, but those migrants blended into the distinctiveness of Creole culture with its Catholicism, ties to family, language traditions, and unique cuisine.

8

"I Don't Remember Her
Going Out to Any Public Places"

A 1925 advertisement in the *New Orleans Herald* read:

WHY NOT A PICTURE OF THE CHILD
With the First Book Bag, on the Way to
School for the First Time
Preserve That Wonderful Event
BERTRAND'S STUDIO
I Like to Make Pictures of Children[1]

Despite any objections her husband may have had to her working as a photographer, Florestine had been running her own studio for at least five years by the time this ad ran. After launching her business in her living room on St. Peter Street, she moved the studio to a commercial space on North Claiborne Avenue where she and her husband lived upstairs. But with each passing day, her unhappy marriage was going from bad to worse. Bertrand's jealousy made him reluctant to allow Florestine the freedoms she longed for. She could not go out so she brought her public to her. Women having "public studios" in the home did not offend idealized views of female domesticity.

White and black women had been encouraged for many years—although for very different reasons—to take up photography. As early as the late 1880s, Eastman Kodak Company founder George Eastman targeted his company's advertising at "the leisured middle-class woman with money to spend on things such as cameras, and time to devote to the technique."[2] These women increasingly turned from taking amateur snapshots to making professional photographs.

Consequently, a substantial number of white women became photographers by the beginning of the twentieth century.[3] In 1900, only 17 women photographers were black. This number swelled to 101 in 1920.[4] While photography was initially marketed to white women as an appropriate feminine pastime, the *Colored American Magazine* asked its female readers as early as 1902 to consider becoming photographers because it was a potentially lucrative occupation.

"The whites do not solicit our patronage; therefore a good opening stands ready for us," wrote the magazine's editor, W. W. Holland. "A little Kodak, a small developing outfit, and a few pennies worth of material will give you a start."[5]

Bertrand's low-paying menial job may have motivated Florestine to start a photography business to increase their family income. In the ten years they were married, he was variously employed as a driver, peddler, or iceman. Bertrand was fortunate to be employed at all given that, at the turn of the century, "black male employment dropped even in 'Negro jobs.' One of the clearest signs" of the precariousness of black male employment, historian William H. Harris writes, "was the decreasing number of black draymen, teamsters, and hack men in the South."[6] "All business places had their horses and wagons before the automobile age, and drivers averaged ten dollars a week," Florestine's friend Jeannette Warburg Altimus said. As a result of their husbands' low wages, as historian Stephanie J. Shaw explains, "between 1890 and 1954, few black women were relieved of the necessity of earning an income."[7]

Since the overwhelming majority of white photographers would not make photographs of African Americans, Florestine benefitted from word of mouth and her ads in newspapers and listings in black business directories. Winifred Hall Allen, whose studio was in Harlem, appears to be one of the few African American women photographers who made pictures outside of her studio in the 1930s.[8] For the most part, making pictures of public events such as banquets, fraternal society picnics, or athletic contests at local schools would remain a male domain for many years.

Florestine used her friend Jeannette Warburg Altimus as a practice model, draping her in pearls in one photo (photo 20). She also typed letters to pastors of Catholic parishes to get the names of children making their "big communion." Florestine would meet with priests to follow up on her letters. "We went to one white church," explained Altimus, "and the old preacher was so mad, he wouldn't come downstairs. He didn't want to be bothered. But other churches would give the list, and then I would type the cards to the parents." Florestine offered them a package of large and small photographs as well as postcards of the communicants. First Communions were Florestine's bread and butter. "I don't remember her

Photo 20. Jeannette Warburg, practice model, early 1920s.

Photo 21. Arthé C. Perrault, Florestine's niece, First Communion, 1936. By permission of Arthé Perrault Anthony.

going out to any big public places," Altimus said. In 1936, Florestine photographed my mother when she was eight years old and dressed for her confirmation. She is wearing a white dress made by *modiste* Louise Barrois, holding a missal and rosary, and wearing a small veil (photo 21). Another communicant's photo is of a boy also dressed in white standing next to a column, one of Florestine's many props (photo 22). She also continued to take pictures of babies and young people, including an unidentified baby boy (photo 23). And she later made a photograph of Beverly

Photo 22. Unidentified communicant, early 1940s.

Photo 23. Unidentified baby
boy, 1940s.

Bart, the daughter of a family friend, wearing curls in 1940 when she was twelve
years old (photo 24).

It is clear that in this period, portrait photography became increasingly attractive to African Americans. The portrait of another unidentified woman demon-
strates the emphasis she placed on dignity and respectability (photo 25). One of
Florestine's self-portraits with her holding a bunch of flowers and wearing a trendy
hairstyle projects the image that she, too, is a modern urban woman (photo 26).
Familiarity with photography and the ensuing popularity of portrait studios are

Photo 24. Beverly Bart with curls, 1940. By permission of Beverly Bart Broyard.

Photo 25. Unidentified woman, late 1920s. The Historic New Orleans Collection, accession no. 2001.79.3.

Photo 26. Florestine Perrault Bertrand, self-portrait with flowers, ca. mid-1920s.

in part attributable to the impact of consumer culture on black communities. Harlem residents who sat for the well-known photographer James VanDerZee mimicked "poses found in contemporary magazine images, especially in the publications devoted to fashion, cinema, and the new activity of celebrity watching."[9] Florestine and other black photographers had similar experiences with customers who wanted contemporary poses to reflect their awareness of the latest trends. Florestine's photograph of her fashionably dressed younger sister Mildred shows off her painted fingernails (plate 4).

Florestine was keenly aware of commercial photography's broad appeal when she expanded her business in the 1920s. In addition to the letters, postcards, and newspaper ads, she also took advantage of the many—albeit often short-lived— black business directories and special publications that highlighted the accomplishments of the city's entrepreneurs. Following World War I, black businesses stood as tangible evidence of African American talent and progress, further demonstrating black entitlement to full citizenship rights in the era of the New Negro movement's spirit of optimism. The New Negro represented accomplishment and pride, a point of view that rejected second-class status. This philosophy was a central tenet of the Harlem Renaissance, a period in which arts and literature of the Negro flourished and were seen as demonstrating black intelligence and a distinctive aesthetic. That optimism is reflected in an unidentified photographer's portrait of Florestine projecting her self-confident sense of style, beauty, and sexuality (photo 27).

Heralding black success and capability in the early decades of the twentieth century did little, however, to reduce the heightened racial tension and violence that characterized those years. A case of mistaken identity in New Orleans in 1900 spiraled out of control when Robert Charles, a black man, shot twenty-seven white men after an encounter with police.[10] Two decades later, the largest number of race riots took place nationwide during the "Red Summer" of 1919. These events punctuated "the greatest period of interracial strife the nation had ever witnessed," writes scholar John Hope Franklin.[11] And although historians often comment on the decline of lynching in the South in the 1920s, the February 1923 issue of the *Survey* magazine reported that Louisiana had the highest number of lynchings in the country between 1889 and 1922.[12]

In that climate of racial repression, African Americans nonetheless continued their fight for first-class citizenship, campaigning for their right to vote. Black women in New Orleans and throughout Louisiana worked against the state's negrophobic white women's suffrage movement. These black women—many of whom Florestine knew—registered to vote and joined civic, religious, and social organizations devoted to advancement of the race.

Photo 27. Florestine Perrault Collins in the Roaring Twenties (late 1920s). Unidentified photographer.

"Photography Requires Nimble Fingers"

At the turn of the twentieth century, women commercial portraitists—regardless of race—were expected to complement and not challenge traditional views of femininity and domesticity.[1] At the same time, African American women photographers had the additional responsibility of reflecting race pride in the photographs they made. In an article in the *Colored American*, W. W. Holland implored middle-class African American women to learn photography because of what he characterized as their refinement.

"You who are teachers and leaders must know good pictures and must be able to select the best and help your neighbors to do the same or else you will fail to do the best part of the work allotted to you," Holland wrote. He argued that black women had a social responsibility for the betterment of the race to rectify this perceived tragic state of affairs by applying their special talents to the growing field of photography.

Holland considered women as having inherent qualities that suited them to become photographers. "Photography requires nimble fingers and hands that are not clumsy, artistic taste, love for beauty and neatness," he wrote. "These qualities combined in the proper proportions are what every woman should have, and all photographers must have."[2] Although Holland's remarks were meant to flatter, they reflect values that may have inhibited many women from developing their talents to the fullest extent and, in the case of photographers, from choosing subjects that were considered less than feminine.

Despite the pervasiveness of such attitudes about femininity, many "black women began to challenge male views concerning feminine roles in American society," explains Cynthia Neverdon-Morton in *Afro-American Women of the South and the Advancement of the Race, 1895–1925*.[3] But in African American communities, challenging gender roles did not mean challenging "femininity."

"Consequently," literary historian Claudia Tate explains, "like white Americans, black Americans increasingly associated social prosperity with the Victorian family model of male assertiveness and female reticence and leisure . . . for the wife and other females of the household. . . . [M]odesty and reserve were essential . . . components in this formula."[4] One photograph made in the very early 1920s of Daisy Fuller demurely posing with flowers illustrates the emphasis placed on those ladylike qualities (photo 28).

Historian Lynn Dumenil argues that while there were "complex changes which transformed and in many ways modernized women's lives . . . for most women, the modern goals of equality and personal autonomy were often elusive."[5] Women's job choices were extremely limited in the 1920s. This was particularly true for black women. Eighty-six percent of white women "were clustered in ten occupations."[6] Black women's jobs, despite African American women's migration to the North in search of more opportunities than menial work, continued to be the least desirable and lowest paid. Florestine avoided those jobs when, in 1920, she became one of three women photographers in New Orleans. This small number may be indicative of how difficult it was for southern women to successfully challenge traditional gender roles in the early decades of the twentieth century. This difficulty persisted despite the creation of what at the time were unique job opportunities available primarily to individual white women during the World War I era.

When a white woman was employed in a nontraditional job in New Orleans, it was such a curiosity that it was frequently noted in one of the daily newspapers. For example, a September 1918 story in the *New Orleans Daily Picayune* reported that Catherine Carval was "the first lady booking agent clerk to be appointed in the New Orleans motion picture territory." Carval "has the charge of dating and shipping films for the Consolidated Film Exchange," the story said, and her selection was war-related, given the manpower shortage. Another example of the attention given to white women who ventured into new territory was the unusual and, therefore, newsworthy appointment of a female mail carrier in Opelousas. The white press, however, paid virtually no attention to African Americans except to paint them as nefarious or as criminals.

Florestine's photography studio was not listed in the 1920 city directory, but we know from a variety of sources that she was in business for herself at a time when more than seven thousand white women in this country were identified as photographers. The tremendous disparity between the experiences of white and black women photographers is not surprising given the discrimination that African American women experienced in all sectors of the economy. And it is possible that some of those white women who were listed as photographers by

Photo 28. Daisy Fuller, Florestine's friend, with flowers, very early 1920s. Direct positive.

the 1920 census were actually wage laborers employed,[7] or in some instances exploited, by large photography concerns as photo finishers or retouchers in cities such as Chicago or New York. While limited job choices—as well as poor wages and unpleasant working conditions—affected all working women, racial prejudice further narrowed black women's occupations.

Florestine's first listing in the city directory as a photographer came in 1923, after she had moved her studio and household—which included her husband and eighteen-year-old Jeannette—to the combined commercial and residential space on North Claiborne in the city's downtown Fifth Ward. Daisy Fuller and Jeannette pose seated on the front steps of Bertrand's Studio in its new location with the showcases behind them (photo 29). Florestine's reputation as a photographer and her business success continued growing as she found ways to assert her independence despite the efforts of her husband, Eilert, to control her.

She was able to focus her energies on her studio because her widowed maternal grandmother, Octavie Jules, known as "Ma mère," arrived daily to prepare the Bertrands' dinner and help with other housekeeping chores. This pattern may have begun early in Florestine's marriage because, as Jeannette recalled, "she didn't know how to cook or nothing like that." When "Ma mère" died at seventy-four years of age in 1932, Florestine's mother, Emilie, assumed those responsibilities. Florestine photographed her grandmother in the late 1920s when she was full of years (photo 30).

The support of her grandmother—and later her mother—bolstered Florestine's confidence about her ability to run her own business and manage many of her domestic responsibilities. The supportive involvement of these older women, first assisting Florestine as a new wife and later as a photographer and businesswoman who worked long hours, is evidence of the network of family and friends encircling her throughout her career and for the rest of her long life. Both of her sisters, Mildred and Thelma, played important roles in her business, especially when she relocated to South Rampart Street in the mid-1930s.

Photo 29. Jeannette Warburg (*left*) and Daisy Fuller on the steps of Florestine's studio, mid-1920s.

Photo 30. Octavie Jules, Florestine's grandmother, late 1920s.

"Persistent Yearnings to Be Free"

Harlem was boiling over with ideas and art in the 1920s. African American intellectual Alain Locke had proclaimed the arrival of the New Negro in his now-famous essay. "The younger generation is vibrant with a new psychology; the new spirit is awake in the masses," he wrote.[1] Langston Hughes, Zora Neale Hurston, W.E.B. Du Bois, and dozens of other writers, artists, and musicians were challenging white America's perception of the Negro and reshaping the Negro's perception of himself. The Harlem Renaissance was swelling to a crescendo. The Negro, as Hughes put it, "was in vogue."[2]

That may have been the case in intellectual centers like New York. Most of the country took little note of the New Negro. Even before Harlem became a cauldron of creative expression, D. W. Griffith had scored a blow for race hatred in 1915 with the release of his film *Birth of a Nation* glorifying the Ku Klux Klan. Ten years later, thirty thousand Klansmen would march down Pennsylvania Avenue in Washington in a show of force and demonstration of public acceptance of its white supremacist ideology. Race remained the determinant, the dominant thread in the American social fabric. And it had received legal underpinnings in 1896, when the U.S. Supreme Court ruled against New Orleans Creole Homère Patrice (Homer) Plessy in *Plessy v. Ferguson*, legalizing state-mandated racial segregation and establishing the fiction of "separate but equal." Jim Crow had become the law of the land.

So were the Thirteenth, Fourteenth, and Fifteenth Amendments to the U.S. Constitution, but they had virtually no impact on opening the polling booths to black voters after they were disfranchised in the decades following the collapse of Reconstruction in 1877. Every ploy imaginable was used to keep black voting to a minimum—poll taxes, literacy tests, exams on the most arcane sections of the Constitution. In 1920, 2,599 African Americans were registered to vote in New

Orleans, and the overwhelming majority of them were women. But by 1926, only 156 black women were registered. To put those numbers into perspective, in 1922, 598 blacks were registered to vote in comparison to 191,789 white Louisianans.[3]

So opposed were white Louisianans to extending the franchise to black voters that Kate Gordon, the state's leading woman's suffragist, would not support a federal constitutional amendment giving women the right to vote for fear that a federal law would open up voting to African Americans. She wanted suffrage to be adopted by individual state legislatures, thus ensuring that southern states would be able to continue disfranchising African Americans. Gordon, who led the fight for state suffrage, was "the most outspokenly negrophobic of the prominent southern suffragists," writes historian Pamela Tyler. Gordon actively opposed African American male participation in the electoral process and toward that end fought against the federal suffrage amendment.[4] Gordon's reactionary and racist leadership and the influence of antisuffragists in the state "all combined to keep [white] Louisiana women of the 1920s away from politics to a considerable degree."[5] Given this highly charged atmosphere, the limited and declining number of black women and men who were registered voters in the city and state in the 1920s is not surprising.

By the 1920s, black women throughout the country had been actively engaged in the debates over female suffrage for many decades. Historian Darlene Clark-Hine's analysis of black women's political activism even prior to the Civil War provides a historical context for interpreting the 1920s. She writes that because black women's "religious orientation was toward spiritual liberation and personal autonomy, suffrage . . . became the political expression of their persistent yearnings to be free." In the early decades of the twentieth century, black women maintained that tradition by voting in significant numbers wherever they were able to do so.[6]

Florestine did not register to vote until 1947, although several members of her intimate circle were registered as early as the 1920s and 1930s. This included twenty-four-year-old Daisy Fuller—who was a schoolteacher—and her older brother Walter, Florestine's former beau, all of whom were registered to vote as Republicans in 1927. In addition, Florestine's younger brothers Herman (1905–1986) and Arthur (1900–1960) (photo 31), who were both bricklayers, and Arthur's wife, Gladys (1902–1983) (photo 32), were also registered to vote as Republicans that year. Their decisions to register in 1927 may have been spurred by the initiative of the San Jacinto Social and Pleasure Club, a downtown Creole male club that "invited the Orleans Parish registrar of voters to explain the registration procedures" to the group.[7]

Scholar Adam Fairclough writes that the registrar's condescension on that particular occasion inspired the formation of several black civic organizations, including the important downtown Seventh Ward League formed that year and the

Photo 31. Arthur J. Perrault, Florestine's brother, mid-1920s.

Photo 32. Gladys Williams Perrault, Florestine's sister-in-law, mid-1920s.

citywide Federation of Civic Leagues that started in 1929. In this era of poll taxes and literacy tests, the city's newly formed black civic organizations and the local branch of the NAACP, formed in 1915, worked tirelessly with minimal impact to challenge disfranchisement and discrimination.[8]

Although it was extraordinarily difficult for blacks to register to vote between 1922 and 1926, black women who lived in downtown wards—the neighborhoods where Florestine and many of her associates and customers resided—were among those who did vote. An examination of fifty-nine of those female registrants who were living in those wards provides an interesting and varied picture of the types of women who were eager to vote, and serves as examples of black women's determination to do so. Most of the women in this sample were born in Louisiana, and their ages ranged from twenty-three to seventy-nine. Among this group were sixteen housewives, thirteen teachers, four midwives, three dressmakers/seamstresses, two stenographer/clerks, one registered nurse, and eleven who worked in personal service. These women strike me as particularly impressive for both their ordinariness as, for instance, housewives and domestics, and their courage to register to vote. They were all registered as Republicans because they had no other choice, given the Democratic Party's exclusion of black voters from the primaries.

It is possible that Florestine was at least acquainted with some of the downtown black female registrants even if they were outside of her immediate social circle during those years. She may have met and made portraits of Norma Ferguson, a twenty-seven-year-old dressmaker, or forty-six-year-old Estelle Hubbard, who was a registered nurse and later became president of the Louisiana Association of Colored Graduate Nurses. They were confident women and may well have wanted to have their portraits made by an equally successful woman. When Lucille Broussard registered to vote in 1922, she was a housewife living in the Seventh Ward with her husband, Albert, a laborer and member of the Seventh Ward Civic League. The chances that Florestine had at least a passing acquaintance with Lucille and her husband are great because by the 1920s he had been a long-standing member of Central Congregational United Church of Christ, an institution that would become increasingly important to Florestine throughout her adult life. The church held particular meaning for her because her good friends the Fullers were members as early as the 1910s, when Florestine boarded with them. And between 1919 and 1921, Daisy and Walter Fuller's mother served on the church's boards of deaconesses and trustees. She was also a member of the nominating committee for church officers and the social service committee. Florestine had tremendous affection and respect for Mrs. Fuller, whose involvement in Central's leadership may well have inspired her to join.

In the late 1920s, a number of forums on political issues important to black people were held at Central Congregational Church. In 1929, for example, "an educational mass meeting" to discuss implementing a literacy campaign was held at the church "under the auspices of the Federated Civic Leagues," an important downtown black political group.[9] At that meeting, Dr. Joseph A. Hardin, president of the league, spoke about the relationship between literacy and full citizenship rights. The work of men like Hardin, attorney A. P. Tureaud, and George Labat, a laborer, and others engaged in the battle against racial discrimination, as well as their participation in Republican Party politics, was often reported in the *Louisiana Weekly* and other black newspapers. In addition, articles and editorials in the Seventh Ward Civic League's magazine, *Civic Leader (A Magazine for the Better Kind)*, highlighted crucial civil rights issues such as the importance of paying poll taxes along with other strategies for combating black exclusion from the voting booth. An October-November 1929 essay in the *Civic Leader* by George Labat, for example, forcefully argued that white primaries and similar discriminatory practices "were enacted solely to disfranchise our race and eliminate us from politics."[10]

Black women were also actively involved in civil rights. A 1930 composite group photograph made by Villard Paddio of forty-six members of the Seventh Ward Civic League includes twelve women (photo 33). Although men held the public leadership roles in the city's black civil rights organizations, women demonstrated their interest in politics and the well-being of the community in a variety of ways such as, for instance, through their work as teachers, nurses, and social workers. This was a period when merely registering to vote was a bold political act.

Florestine would have been introduced to working-class politics through the union activism of her father, Theophile. Registered to vote in 1931, Theophile was a long-standing member and frequent officer of the racially segregated Bricklayers Union, Louisiana Local Number One, as were other male members of his family. His union activism was not unique because by the early decades of the twentieth century, many black men in New Orleans—especially dock workers—had long been involved in the city's often volatile labor movement. And although many elite black men and women throughout the country were hostile toward organized labor, black union men, as historian Eric Arnesen explains, were often at the forefront of protests against discriminatory practices in New Orleans's segregated economy.

The Bricklayers Union met in the Pythian Temple on Saratoga Street, a building owned by the African American chapter of the Knights of Pythias, a fraternal order. Meetings at this building would have exposed the Perrault men to a broad range of labor issues because of the diverse groups and businesses with offices

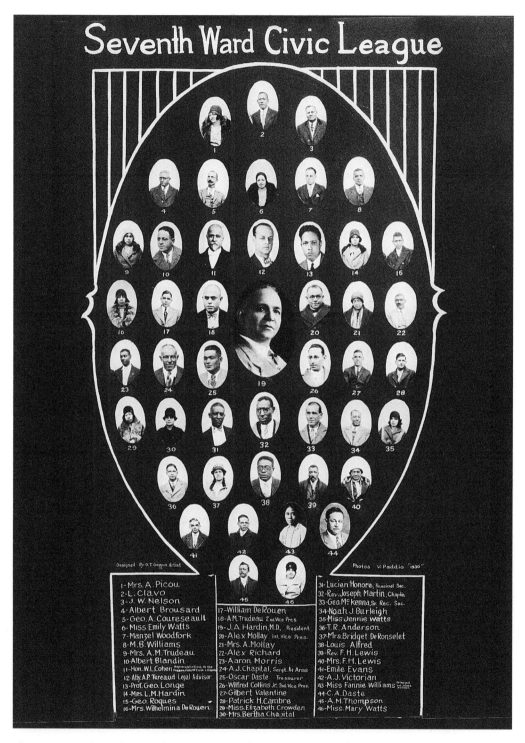

Photo 33. Seventh Ward Civic League, 1930. Joseph A. Hardin Papers. By permission of Amistad Research Center at Tulane University.

there, including the screwmen's, carriage drivers, and hod carriers unions. The Knights of Pythias and the black-owned Liberty Industrial Life Insurance Company, along with the offices of several black professionals including dentists and an attorney, were also housed there.

Beginning in her childhood, Florestine's father was a dedicated 33rd Degree Mason and grand chancellor secretary general of the Supreme Council of Louisiana, an office he would hold for more than thirty years. The ideals of freemasonry—fraternity, service, community—no doubt shaped Florestine's life in what were probably very subtle ways. She photographed George Longe, also a 33rd Degree Mason, wearing the regalia of his office around his neck (photo 34). Black participation in French Republicanism influenced Scottish Rite Freemasonry in New Orleans, and by the 1920s, Freemasonry was an integral part of male Creole culture. As a result, Creole free men of color—many of whom were Catholic in name only—became Masons in significant numbers as early as the beginning of the antebellum period. Many Creole men chose Masonry as an alternate religion, favoring it over Catholicism because of the church's support of slavery and then racial segregation.[11]

As a Mason and union man, Florestine's father exemplified the tradition of independent thinking that characterized black Creole male elites of previous generations. At the same time, increasingly modernist views such as secularization shaped Freemasonry in the 1920s, which locates Theophile Perrault within the dynamics of a modern urban milieu.[12]

Freemasonry may have had a more pragmatic influence on Florestine's approach to entrepreneurship given her father's organizational skills and experience as a lodge officer. As grand chancellor secretary general of his lodge, Theophile corresponded extensively with Masons throughout the world. The voluminous Supreme Council correspondence includes his inquiries in the 1940s to consulates, including those of Cuba and Haiti and countries in western Europe, about their practices. Theophile's responsibilities—and the fact that his lodge was meticulous about record keeping—may have set an example for Florestine about the importance of conducting business in an orderly fashion.

Masons prided themselves on a universalist interpretation of religion that allowed for "broad tolerance and respect for individual conscience," explains Dumenil.[13] While I do not want to overstate the impact of Freemasonry's philosophies on Florestine's values, much later in life she joined the United Church of Religious Science, a New Thought religion founded in 1927 that embraces a philosophy of universalism quite similar to Masonry's interpretation of universality.

Photo 34. George Longe, 1940s. George Longe Papers. By permission of Amistad Research Center at Tulane University.

Three Prominent Creole Photographers

Three prominent Creole photographers emerged in New Orleans in the 1920s: Arthur P. Bedou, Villard Paddio, and Florestine. Bedou, Booker T. Washington's personal photographer, had the most distinguished career of the three. He and Florestine taught Paddio, who used a World War I pension to finance his education before he opened his own studio. Both men had clear advantages over Florestine because they were able to photograph public events and travel outside New Orleans, while Florestine, for the most part, was limited to what she could shoot in her studio. A woman working outside the home was still frowned upon.

Bedou, a talented portraitist and landscapist, describes himself as New Orleans's leading photographer in a 1935 newspaper ad, noting that he had won a gold medal at the Jamestown Exposition in 1907. Photography historian Deborah Willis calls Bedou an artist and journalist best known for documenting Washington's public and private lives. Although he has been dead for decades, he is still remembered by many older Creole New Orleanians for the painstaking care with which he photographed his subjects. I have often heard, "Don't be a Bedou," an expression still used by older Creoles to urge a photographer to hurry up and make a photograph.

Bedou's work was widely known in Creole and African American New Orleans because his photos regularly turned up in the local black newspaper, the *Louisiana Weekly*. A portrait he made of Vivian Dejoie, wife of the *Weekly*'s publisher, and her baby son was published on the cover of a 1916 issue of the NAACP's magazine the *Crisis* that featured black progress in New Orleans. Bedou also made photographs for black organizations such as the National Baptist Convention, National Negro Business League, and National Medical Association. He took on assignments at colleges throughout the South and was eagerly sought after to photograph activities of the People's Life Insurance Company, of which he was an officer, and the Knights of St. Peter Claver, a black male Catholic society. His range included sporting events, cultural programs at local schools, and distinguished visitors to the city.

Florestine had practically no opportunities to photograph newsworthy public events. However, Bedou's photos of her occasionally made the pages of the *Louisiana Weekly*. A March 1934 photograph Bedou made of Florestine and Mae Fuller Keller as "real pals" appeared on the newspaper's front page, with a caption noting that Keller was visiting from Los Angeles and Florestine was a "popular" downtown photographer."[1] Florestine's reputation was local. Bedou's work expanded beyond Creole family and community life. He made distinguished portraits of Booker T. Washington and George Washington Carver, but he also photographed white philanthropists such as steel tycoon Andrew Carnegie and Sears, Roebuck and Company's Julius Rosenwald.

Bedou lived in downtown New Orleans on Bienville Street in the 1920s. He and Florestine were members of the same social circle. She was friends with his wife, Lillia Toledano Bedou, and they belonged to a bridge club, Entre Nous, that Florestine helped to organize. Despite this familiarity, Florestine and Bedou were competitors. The bridge club had Bedou shoot a group picture, but Florestine, upset that she was not asked to make the portrait, refused to be included in the shot. Even seventy years later, Florestine's friend Marguerite Perez vividly recalled how angry she was that she was not chosen as the group's photographer.

Paddio became the third member of this trio in the mid-1920s. Bedou was Paddio's first teacher, but they parted ways due to a disagreement of undetermined origin. Their breakup brought Paddio to Bertrand's Studio for instruction from Florestine, much to her husband's consternation. Paddio became an accomplished portraitist as illustrated by his photograph of Dr. L. T. Burbridge, the president of Louisiana Industrial Life Insurance Company, which appeared on the cover of *Negro American Magazine* in July 1931. And his charming photograph of nautically dressed four-year-old Willie Joseph Misshore was the cover illustration for the August 1932 issue of the local *Our Youth* magazine. In addition to portraits of Creole family and community life, Paddio often made group photographs of musicians. One of his most famous subjects was Louis Armstrong, who called Paddio his favorite photographer when he was at home in the Crescent City.

Florestine did venture out when working with Paddio to make photographs for the 1925 *Crescent City Pictorial: A Souvenir, Dedicated to the Progress of the Colored Citizens of New Orleans*. Priced at fifty cents, the *Pictorial* included two photographs of the Lions Club she signed as "Bertrand." Members of this fraternal and civic organization appeared on one of the *Pictorial*'s pages posing in their uniforms in front of their clubhouse. Included with these two exterior shots is a portrait, made by Florestine or Paddio, of the organization's president, R. J. Llopis (photo 35). Additional unattributed photographs include shots of Florestine in her studio preparing to make a photograph of a young boy. There is also a photograph of her as an exemplar of black progress in New Orleans (photo 36).

Florestine and Paddio made photographs of businesses housed in the Temple, including the offices of doctors Andrew J. Young Sr. and L. J. Gomez. There were also shots of the Liberty Industrial Insurance Company and of members of the Masonic order. In addition, Florestine and Paddio made photographs of the Temple's theater and Roof Garden, the popular location for Saturday dances. Florestine and her friends may have danced there to music performed by bands such as the well-known Manuel Perez Orchestra, whose members included Osceola Blanchard, whom Florestine knew. The Temple also had an auditorium where dances were held (photo 37). Another group of interesting photographs includes scenes of the trimming, embalming, and showrooms of Geddes & Moss

Photo 35. Lions Club, *Crescent City Pictorial*, 1925. O.C.W. Taylor Papers. By permission of Amistad Research Center at Tulane University.

Photo 36. *Crescent City Pictorial* featuring Bertrand's Studio, 1925. O.C.W. Taylor Papers. By permission of Amistad Research Center at Tulane University.

Undertaking & Embalming Company. This was one of the few black businesses in downtown New Orleans in which a woman, Gertrude Geddes Willis, the company's president for many years, played a major role.

As we know, the vast majority of Florestine's work was confined to her studio, which suggests that gender and race shaped her career in the 1920s. This pattern conformed to the experiences of white women photographers at the turn of the twentieth century, when it was extremely unusual to find these women outside of their studios photographing, for instance, urban street life. Although there were exceptions to this general pattern, white women photographers avoided street life as a subject because it "was off limits to most women (with or without a camera), since they were not supposed to appear unaccompanied in city streets." Photography historian Naomi Rosenblum goes on to explain, "Besides the usual fears of being accosted by strange men or coming face to face with prostitutes, there was the problem of attracting too much attention to get the work done."[2] Given

Photo 37. Pythian Temple Auditorium, ca. 1922–23. By permission of Hogan Jazz Archive at Tulane University.

Florestine's early introduction to professional photography, her understanding of appropriate subjects for women photographers might have been shaped by those Victorian values that lingered in a changing American society.

But racial prejudice also affected her career and those of other African American women photographers, given that by the time Florestine went into business, only white "women were being offered jobs in photography to work in museums, medical and technical institutes, newspapers and periodicals, advertising, and government agencies."[3] This was not an era when African American women photographers would experience similar advances. Consequently, black women photographers like Florestine were confined to working as commercial portraitists in segregated African American communities from the 1910s to the 1940s. In this era, black women most often worked in studios run by husband and wife that were, according to Rosenblum's assessment, "relatively unsophisticated ventures."[4]

Many white women also had the luxury of studying art abroad, which had become de rigueur for middle-class white women with interests in art and photography in the early decades of the twentieth century. With the exception of rare examples such as the sculptors Edmonia Lewis (ca. 1845–1911) and Meta Warrick Fuller (1877–1968), who studied in Europe, black women lacked the means to finance study abroad and were excluded from elite art institutions in the United States. An art education and access to photographic circles were crucial to the development of many white women photographers as demonstrated by the experiences of Frances Benjamin Johnston and Gertrude Käsebier. These two well-known early photographers "acquired art backgrounds at prestigious institutions in the United States and in Europe," according to photography historian C. Jane Gover, and they "consistently stressed the significance of that experience to their photography."[5] Johnston, for example, studied in Paris at the *Academie Julian* in the mid-1880s, as Maria Elizabeth Ausherman notes.[6]

The doors of coed camera clubs were also closed to black women, excluding them from membership in groups that "provided encouragement and artistic reinforcement for members."[7] Participation in those informal networks "provided facilities often unobtainable by the amateur or even by the new professional."[8] Hardly any black women, however, would have expected these clubs to welcome them. These networks may have existed in New Orleans in the 1910s and 1920s for white women photographers such as Ruth Hubbard or Alberta Fischer. Between 1916 and 1918, only Hubbard—whose studio was on St. Roch Avenue—was listed as a woman photographer in the business section of the New Orleans city directory. In 1920, and again in 1922, Fischer appears in the directory as having a business located at 829 Canal Street. However, it is important to note that all women photographers, regardless of race, frequently worked in partnership with their brothers, fathers, or husbands, and therefore were often underrepresented in city directories.

In addition to being excluded from opportunities to improve their talents, black women engaged in nontraditional professions also had to contend with their communities' standards of femininity. For Florestine—who was guarded by a jealous first husband—the end result was an inability to work regularly outside of her studio to make photographs of the organizational and public life of black New Orleanians. At times, individual black women, including spirited businesswomen like Florestine, must have chafed against those paternalistic restrictions. The imposition of limits on the careers of black women photographers is particularly ironic given W. W. Holland's early-twentieth-century observations about African American women's suitability for the profession.

Negotiating both the boundaries of female gender roles and white racial prejudice, Florestine relied on her family and friends to refine her skills and expand her business. For example, her two girlfriends Daisy Young (1902–1989) and Jeannette

Warburg Altimus were always willing models as Florestine tried new poses or darkroom techniques. Her father and brother helped put together Florestine's early photographic equipment and darkrooms. She was not unique in this regard because other black women photographers of her day depended on family members and worked within family and community networks.

By the time New Orleans's trio of black photographers—Florestine, Bedou, and Paddio—were seasoned professionals, the distinction between art and commercial photography was well established. But from the 1920s to the 1930s, the artistic and technical quality of southern black photographers' work went unnoticed outside of the segregated communities they served. A handful, however, such as New Yorker James Latimer Allen, were recognized for their work—although as Negroes of accomplishment and not as photographers per se. During the Harlem Renaissance Latimer Allen received the William E. Harmon Award for Distinguished Achievement among Negroes. Other black photographers presented their work in art exhibitions organized, for instance, by the Department of Negro Literature and History in the well-known 135th Street branch of the New York Public Library in Harlem.

Probably the most accomplished black photographer on the national scene was Addison Scurlock of Washington, D.C., who opened his studio in 1911. His photographs featured the African American elite and institutional life in Washington, D.C., and throughout the South. His work was published in national black magazines including A. Philip Randolph and Chandler Owen's socialist magazine, the *Messenger*, the Urban League's *Opportunity*, and the NAACP's *Crisis*. Scurlock's interests—many of which were later shared by his two sons, who joined the business in the 1930s—were extraordinarily diverse for a black photographer at that time. For example, he made motion pictures and newsreels between 1948 and 1952, and his two sons operated a photography school whose pupils included future photojournalists.

In New Orleans, the work of some nationally recognized black photographers was included in the six annual exhibits of black artists held by Dillard University in cooperation with the Harmon Foundation in the 1930s.[9] There is no evidence that Florestine's work was included in this exhibit, which was highly unlikely given her lack of national recognition as a photographer at that time. With the exception of exhibits sponsored by black institutions or organized by white patrons for exclusively black participants, African American photographers were excluded from what Alan Trachtenberg refers to as "the forms of cultural authority."[10] As a result, black photographers had precious few opportunities to exhibit their work and establish reputations in the elite white art world. But despite their being pushed to the utmost margins of mainstream photography, a number of them were able to make their livelihoods by working for their black customers.

"I Met Herbert and Fell in Love with Him"

Florestine gave her business much greater exposure in the early 1920s, when she moved it from her home to North Claiborne near other black businesses in the Tremé neighborhood. The new location allowed her to tap into American consumers' growing familiarity with photography, a consequence of the relative affordability of cameras for hobbyists. Cameras found a place in stores alongside a wide selection of popular items from watches to radios, from bicycles to ashtrays. As one newspaper advertisement read: "A pocket Kodak, Series II, is sure to make a hit with anyone—reason enough for our suggesting it for Christmas."

By the 1920s, the range of cameras for sale varied from the relatively expensive Kodak Series II, which cost from $13.50 to $26.00, to the $1.70 "Little Brownie." As an indication of how commonplace cameras had become, a drugstore advertised cameras in the *Times Picayune* along with such traditional Christmas gift items as boxes of candy, perfume, and cigars. Still, cameras were beyond the reach of most African Americans. "In those days everybody didn't have a camera like they have now," collector Teresa Sidle Hardeman remembers. Even "a little Kodak," she points out, "was a luxury." Hardeman added about her experiences, "We had school pictures, like when I graduated," revealing the extent to which photographs were relied on to commemorate celebratory moments even during extremely hard times when personal cameras were uncommon in some communities.[1]

Aware of the growing importance of photographs in everyday life, Florestine continued to use newspaper advertisements and direct mail to attract customers in the mid-1920s to the 1930s. In this period, black self-representation in photographs continued to have symbolic meaning as part of efforts of African Americans to construct a modern sense of themselves. Black political leaders, educators, intellectuals, and entrepreneurs were articulating a philosophy of racial advancement and full citizenship rights during the era of the New Negro, continuing the expression of aspirations and demands going back to colonial days.

Photography was important to this effort, with images of dignified and sophisticated African American women, men, children, and families illustrating black publications and on display in proud families' homes as Deborah Willis discusses in her essay "Picturing the New Negro Woman."[2] Portraits reaffirming black dignity often appeared in national magazines such as *Crisis, Golden Thoughts,* the *Colored American*, and the *Brownies Book* as well as in local publications such as New Orleans's *Our Youth* magazine and the *Civic Leader (A Magazine for the Better Kind)*.

Historian Kevin K. Gaines elaborates on the strategic use of photographs as visual weaponry in the struggle against "the cultural dimensions of white supremacy" in *Uplift the Race: Black Leadership, Politics, and Culture in the Twentieth Century*.[3] "Because photography was crucial in transmitting stereotypes, African Americans found the medium well suited for trying to refute negrophobic caricatures," he writes. This is reflected, he argues, in "studio portraits of uplift and respectability—depicting black families with attributes of cleanliness, leisure, and literacy—[that] found expression in the sitters' posture, demeanor, dress, and setting. In most portraits, whether of individuals or groups, one sees an intense concern with projecting a positive image."[4]

Florestine's photography and the expectations of her subjects were influenced by and contributed to this highly politicized visual discourse on racial betterment. Consequently, in addition to a concern for fashion and style, photographers had to be sensitive to the importance of maintaining their customers' dignity in images they captured. However, photographer and subject were not always the sole arbiters of what was dignified. On one occasion in the early 1920s, an enraged father objected to a portrait of his teenage daughter, Nettie George, appearing in Bertrand's Studio's showcase for any passerby to see. He was very upset that the photograph had been put on display (photo 38).

George often visited the Bertrands' home because she was Jeannette Warburg Altimus's good friend and one of Florestine's many beautiful practice models. In the offending pose, Florestine was, according to Altimus, merely practicing how to drape her subjects, but for Mr. George, his daughter's virtue was at stake. That incident most likely served as an invaluable lesson for Florestine about the importance of customer satisfaction as well as getting permission from the appropriate individuals before displaying images.

With experience, Florestine learned to promote her skills to appeal to the personal needs of her customers as demonstrated by her marketing techniques. Her 1925 *New Orleans Herald* ad appeals to mothers with its implication that as

Photo 38. Nettie George, practice model, early 1920s.

a woman photographer, she had special skills for understanding the importance of critical moments in a child's development. Of course, the irony of this is that Florestine did not have children of her own, which is what freed her to devote her energy to being a photographer and an entrepreneur.

Her business may have provided the only escape she had from the deepening unhappiness she felt in her marriage. She may have considered leaving the marriage for any number of reasons, but, as she describes the decisive moment, "I met Herbert and I fell in love with him—that was the end of the marriage" (photo 39). Florestine fell in love with Herbert W. Collins—her husband's best friend—whom she married in 1928. That the Bertrands were friends with Collins lends an air of daring and romantic drama to imagining the attractive Florestine Perrault Bertrand's relationship with Collins.

At times, Altimus remembers, there were tense moments during Florestine and Collins's clandestine courtship. Marrying a family friend was a common pattern in an era when women's public lives were often defined first by their fathers' and then by their husbands' dictates. This reality runs counter to the stereotypes of women's freedoms during the Roaring Twenties. In Bertrand's case, he was intensely jealous of other men, and the only man he trusted with Florestine was Collins. She chose her second husband more wisely than she had her first. Their marriage was successful for twenty-seven years, until Collins's death in 1955, several years after they had moved to Los Angeles for the second time.

Impatient with Louisiana's conservative divorce laws, the couple first moved to Los Angeles in 1927 so Florestine could establish residency to secure a divorce. They chose Los Angeles because Florestine's close friend Mae Fuller Keller had moved there with her husband, George Keller, in the early 1920s. Florestine and Collins soon found jobs in Los Angeles. In order to work in a photographic business, Florestine again passed for white because the job opportunities for African American women in Los Angeles were not much different than in the South in the late 1920s. She recalled working in Glendale, an extremely conservative community known for its hostility toward nonwhites. Florestine did not share any negative stories about her experiences, but she did remember that her wages were at least eighteen dollars a week. Her expenses included the thirty-five cents she paid for carfare in addition to her lunch.

Collins was less fortunate in finding a job and salary commensurate with his skills, experience, and status as a former postal carrier. Due to the limited jobs available to African American men, he accepted work as a laundry truck driver, a job for which he was ill-suited. Although Florestine and Collins first moved to Los Angeles with the intention of making a life there, he was unable to hide

Photo 39. Herbert W. Collins, Florestine's second husband, early 1930s.

his frustration at not finding a decent job. His fruitless search forced them to return to New Orleans. Collins was the first to take the train home after the New Orleans postmaster offered him his former job with the condition that he return right away.

Florestine and Collins clearly were eager to marry, and they did so very shortly after they had both returned to New Orleans. The February 22, 1928, ceremony was performed by a Jefferson Parish justice of the peace and was witnessed by Daisy Fuller, Mae Keller's younger sister. "The reason we got married on the twenty-second of February was because it was a holiday, and he didn't have to work," Florestine said. "I got to New Orleans on Carnival day—I'll never forget that."

The couple married even though California law required that they wait a year before an interlocutory judgment became a final divorce. Louisiana law also required a woman to wait ten months after her divorce before marrying again. Florestine and Collins may have been confused about the distinction between an interlocutory decree and final divorce judgment. It is more reasonable to assume that they simply took advantage of the fact that their trip West sufficiently symbolized to family and friends their fresh start. After a short hiatus from work following her divorce and remarriage, Florestine reopened her studio on North Claiborne. She renamed her business Claiborne Studio, a name she continued to use through the early years of the Great Depression. In 1934, she changed the name again to Collins Studio and moved to South Rampart. In 1947, she moved again only a few blocks away on Rampart.

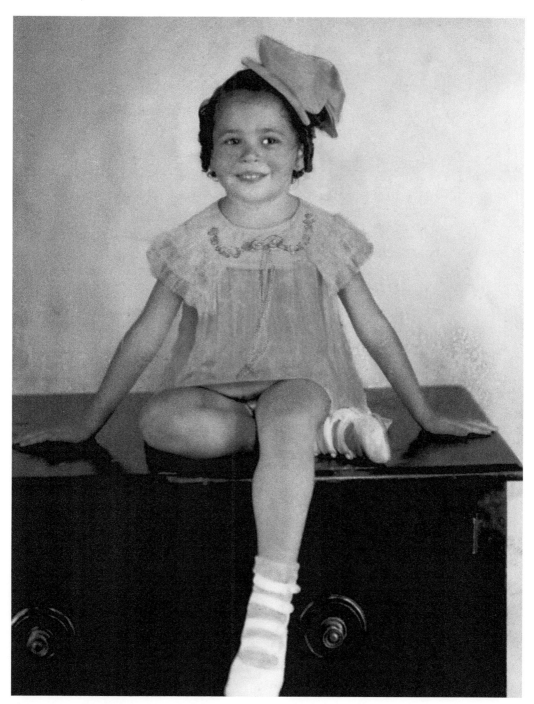

Plate 1. Germaine Gardina, Florestine's niece, as a child, mid-1930s.

Plate 2. Jean and Germaine Gardina as teenagers, mid-1940s.

Plate 3. Lydia Sindos as a junior bridesmaid, 1945. Lydia Sindos Adams Papers. Amistad Research Center at Tulane University.

Plate 4. Mildred Perrault Gardina, Florestine's sister, wearing a hat and with hand-painted fingernails, mid-1930s.

Plate 5. Jeannette Warburg Altimus, Florestine's friend, wearing a hat, late 1920s.

Plate 6. (*left*) Lionel Barthelemy Jr., baby picture, 1937. By permission of Ruth F. Barthelemy.

Plate 7. (*below*) Lorraine McCarthy and Morris Labostrie wedding, 1946. By permission of Sonja McCarthy.

Plate 8. "Boss Lady" Florestine dressed for work, 1930s.

Plate 9. Mae Fuller Keller dressed for Mardi Gras formal dance, mid-1940s.

Plate 10. Bobbie Anderson, a visitor from out of town, mid-1940s.

"Everybody Got All Dressed Up
and Went to the Studio"

On rare occasions, Florestine focused her lens on entertainers like Almo the Fan Dancer, captured in a 1937 shot published in the *Louisiana Weekly*. When Neliska "Baby" Briscoe returned to New Orleans in the mid-1930s, Florestine photographed her sporting a white-jacketed tuxedo and holding a baton (photo 40). After years of professional dancing in New York, Briscoe came home to become "the star attraction of the popular Joe Robichaux's Rhythm Boys Band."[1] Mae Diggs, another New Orleans entertainer, became a well-known singer, dancer, and screen actor in the 1930s and 1940s.[2] Florestine photographed Diggs in 1935 on one of her visits to the city, wearing a hat and flanked by her two nephews, Raymond and Wallace Young (photo 41).

Good friends, their families, and walk-in customers, though, remained the staples of her business. In 1932, one of her dearest friends, Daisy Fuller Young—a former schoolteacher and the wife of the senior Andrew Young, a dentist—brought her oldest son, Andrew, to have a baby picture made (photo 42). The Youngs were secure members of the city's black upper class because they were educated professionals and homeowners as well as Florestine's close personal friends. Daisy was later photographed in 1949 proudly seated with her two sons, Walter and Andrew, standing by her side (photo 43).

As an indication of the widespread appeal of photographs in the 1930s, several studios clustered in black business areas near Florestine, Bedou, and Paddio. The competitors included Mack McCormick's Magnolia Studio, Fernande Wiltz's Union Photo Shop, and Henderson Wright's Studio. Just two blocks from Arthur Bedou's home studio, Frederick McLain opened a studio in the mid-1930s in his home on Bienville Avenue. After McLain and his wife, Adine, divorced, she

Photo 40. Neliska "Baby" Briscoe, mid-1930s. By permission of Hogan Jazz Archive at Tulane University.

Photo 41. Mae Diggs and nephews, 1935. By permission of Sonja McCarthy.

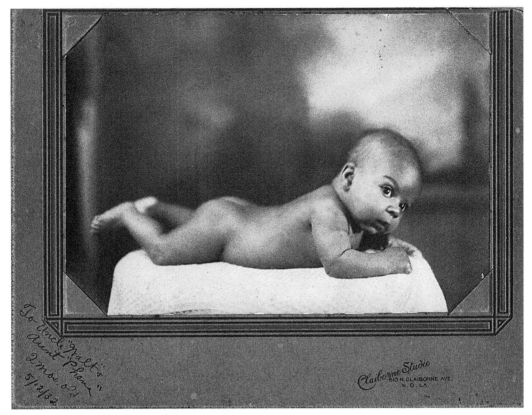

Photo 42. Ambassador Andrew Young as a baby, 1935.

opened her own studio, Camera Masters.[3] Florestine's brother Arthur and his wife, Gladys, opened Perrault's Studio on South Rampart Street in 1936, just a few blocks south of Collins Studio. Going to a photographer's studio "was a big outing," said Florestine's niece Arthé Perrault Anthony. "Everybody got all dressed up and went to the studio."

After Florestine was in business for more than fifteen years, her reputation was well-established. Malcolm Barrois, a former customer, described her as "the photographer of the moment." In 1939, Barrois and his bride, Lynette Gautier, selected Collins Studio to photograph their large wedding party of eight bridesmaids and grooms (photo 44). "Arthur Bedou was considered the master photographer in New Orleans," Barrois said. "But at that time Collins was the photographer of the moment because Bedou had grown older, and she was more in touch with the social life of New Orleans." As the caption for the 1934 photograph "Real Pals" notes, "Collins is a popular photographer from the downtown sector."[4] By moving Collins Studio to South Rampart Street in 1934, Florestine was no longer an exclusively downtown photographer.

Photo 43. Daisy, Walter, and Andrew Young, 1949. Daisy Young Family Papers. By permission of Amistad Research Center at Tulane University.

Delta Shadows: A Pageant of Negro Progress in New Orleans included Collins Studio as one of "several outstanding businesses conducted by Negroes," describing it as "an up-to-the-minute establishment located . . . in the heart of New Orleans's commercial district."[5]

To stay in business when disposable income was hard to come by, photographers frequently had to adjust their prices. Bedou slashed some of his in half. Florestine also responded to her customers' tightening purse strings by making three

Photo 44. Lynnette Gautier and Malcolm J. Barrois wedding, 1939. By permission of Malcolm J. Barrois.

8" × 10" photographs for only one dollar when earlier a single photograph that size cost eighty-nine cents. Competing studios gave black consumers a number of choices. Union Photo and Perrault's studios were located within seven blocks of Collins Studio. They advertised special services such as free enlargements to customers paying for the development of their own Kodak film. Union Photo promoted quick finishing and full-length cards for only ten cents.[6] And some African Americans had begun patronizing white photographers, albeit very infrequently.

When her brother Arthur moved his studio just a couple of blocks away, Florestine did not discourage him. "It didn't make any difference, because the white man was out there, and he was in competition with me," she said. "So I said, 'You go right ahead.'" Arthur had helped his sister by building the booth housing the direct positive camera. He played an important role, Florestine said, but her younger sister Mildred was also extremely helpful from the start.

"I taught her, and I had to teach Arthur," Florestine said. "I had to teach Mildred how to paint. I remember the first day that we opened the studio, we worked so hard the day before, and the night before we were practically up all night getting things together." As her staff expanded, "everybody had to learn . . . as each new girl came along we had to teach them how to paint. . . . Of course, teaching them how to make the pictures wasn't anything because it was all by machine. All they had to do was turn the crank."

Shortly after opening Collins Studio, Florestine also hired Mildred's and Arthur's spouses, Johnny Gardina and Gladys. The economic and social effects of the Depression were widely felt in the city, making employment in a family-owned business a safety net. Florestine hired Gardina, Mildred's first husband, after his Italian American father's grocery store closed, leaving his son without a job. Florestine's youngest sister, Thelma, was the last member of the family to join the staff and worked in sales. Over time, a number of non–family members also worked in the studio full- and part-time in the 1940s.

Before he opened Perrault's Studio in New Orleans, Arthur opened two short-lived photography businesses in Atlanta in 1936. He chose Atlanta, his wife said, because they thought it "was one of the best places for Negro businesses. There were Negroes in banking. There was a Negro newspaper; there were Negroes in all types of work, and there the Negroes believed in patronizing each other. They'd go for blocks and blocks in order to patronize a Negro business." Planning to profit from this spirit and having learned the value of a business's location from working with his sister, Arthur opened his studios on Auburn Avenue, N.E., and Decatur. As early as the turn of the twentieth century, Auburn Avenue was considered "the best-appointed street for Negroes in the city of Atlanta,"[7] and therefore an ideal spot for a colored photographer to work. Black Atlantan Alice Adams's description of the social and symbolic significance of Auburn Avenue for African Americans explains why Arthur and other black entrepreneurs were attracted to the street: "That's where we dressed up, because we couldn't dress up during the day. . . . We'd dress up and put on our good clothes and go to the show on Auburn. And you were going places. It was like white folks' Peachtree."[8]

For blacks who were forced to wear uniforms or other symbols of subservience on their jobs, dressing up symbolized the transformation they underwent when they no longer were at work, where they were expected to be deferential to whites in manner and dress. Dressing up was also part of the preparation associated with having a photograph made. In Atlanta in 1936–37, there were at least five African American photographers, three of whom had studios within two blocks of one another on Auburn Avenue. Although the Perraults were optimistic about Atlanta's promise, they were naïve about the racially charged atmosphere in one of the strongholds of the Ku Klux Klan. Those racial tensions were exacerbated by the economic pressures of the Depression. Consequently, Arthur and Gladys were ill-prepared, as she recalled, for the unfettered expression of white supremacy in the most segregated city in Georgia, and they therefore returned to New Orleans to begin afresh with their own studio first located uptown on Magnolia Street.

"They Came in Droves"

Well aware of New Orleans's racial boundaries, Florestine took her very light-skinned friend Jeannette Warburg Altimus with her when she went to sign the forty-dollar-a-month rental agreement on her South Rampart building. She wanted to encourage the white owner of the property to think he was renting the space to a white woman. A hand-painted photograph of Altimus with a stylish hat illustrates how fair-skinned she was (plate 5). This racial sleight-of-hand most likely made it possible for her to become the first African American entrepreneur with a business at the "gateway" to Rampart Street when it was still in its heyday.

Upon their arrival in New Orleans, African American visitors disembarked from trains servicing the Louisiana and Arkansas Railway Lines (L&A), whose station was on South Rampart. Union Station was only a few blocks farther south. Passengers on the L&A, Gulf Coast, Illinois Central, Southern Pacific, and Yazoo and Mississippi Valley lines could easily find Rampart Street's businesses. It was a lively urban black district, home to a variety of respectable businesses—including three photography studios—as well as seamier venues for dancing, drinking, gambling, and prostitution.

Florestine's customers were people "who knew me or came from Canal Street or went to the shows," she said. "There were two shows there: the Loew's State and the Orpheum. I got the traffic." A great deal of the 1940s traffic came from World War II servicemen and women, including twenty-four-year-old soldier Ulysses H. Gore from Cambridge, Massachusetts. Gore was stationed outside of the city in barracks still under construction. He recalled taking the Carrollton Avenue trolley into the city, where he came across Florestine's studio in 1942. He had photographs made in two poses, sending one to his mother and keeping the other for himself (photo 45). After Gore was shipped overseas, he met a fellow soldier who recognized him from a portrait displayed in Florestine's studio showcase. Florestine also photographed an unidentified merchant marine in 1943, another likely walk-in (photo 46).

Phenella DuPlessis Perez, who worked at Collins on weekends when she was a freshman at Xavier University, remembered taking some of the quick-finish photographs when the studio was extremely busy (photo 47). "The servicemen and soldiers lined up; they came in droves and with their girlfriends, too," she said.

Photo 45. Ulysses H. Gore, in the U.S. Army, 1942. By permission of Ulysses H. Gore.

Photo 46.
Unidentified
merchant marine,
early 1940s.

"We would put a little tint on since there was no color at that time. We painted those with something like little cotton swabs and watercolor." The weekend traffic increased when "the GIs got their paychecks," she said. "Business was booming on the weekends." The quick-finish photographs were popular, Perez said, because "the guys were on the run. They were just passing because they were in the neighborhood." Florestine photographed her brother-in-law Clement Lombard

Photo 47. Phenella DuPlessis as an Xavier University student, 1947. By permission of Phenella DuPlessis Perez.

standing proudly in his Army uniform in the early 1940s (photo 48). A photograph of his wife, Thelma, Florestine's younger sister, wearing trousers was taken around the same time (photo 49). She also made a photograph of John Altimus, her friend Jeannette's husband, in the same period (photo 50).

Customers also included students at two schools run by women. The Martinez Nursery School, the only kindergarten in New Orleans for black children, was a Seventh Ward institution that staged an elaborate annual pageant in addition to a graduation ceremony. Florestine's brother Arthur photographed many of the pageants and graduations at the school. Collins Studio photographed individual

Photo 48. Clement Lombard, Florestine's brother-in-law, in the U.S. Army, early 1940s.

Photo 49. Thelma Perrault Lombard, Florestine's sister, mid-1940s. By permission of Carmelita Perrault Lagarde.

Photo 50. John
Altimus, Jeannette
Warburg's husband,
ca. 1940s.

youngsters who came to her studio dressed in their pageant costumes or graduation caps and gowns. An unidentified girl wears her cap and gown and holds her
diploma from a Martinez School graduation (photo 51). According to Sybil Kein,
Florestine also made pictures for some students at Alma Moore Booker's Dancing
School, who were dressed in costumes to perform in one of the school's revues.
New Orleanians loved pageants and there were many of them such as the fund-
raiser held at the Valena C. Jones Elementary School. Boys and girls competed to

be named king or queen. A 1933 photograph of my mother was taken of her in the first grade wearing an elaborate Louise Barrois costume when my mother hoped to but failed to be selected queen that year (photo 52).

Florestine would continue to take pictures of babies and children in the 1930s, like the one she made of Ferdinand J. Montegut when he was eight months old.

Photo 51. Unidentified girl dressed for graduation from the Martinez School, 1940s. By permission of Numa Martinez.

Photo 52. Arthé C. Perrault dressed for a Valena C. Jones School pageant, 1932. By permission of Arthé Perrault Anthony.

Ruth Barthelemy, the mother of former New Orleans mayor Sidney Barthelemy, said families made two stops following the birth of a baby—the church and the photographer. Florestine made a picture, although not the first one, of Barthelemy's son Lionel Jr. when he was six months old in 1937 (plate 6). An important staple of Florestine's business included group pictures such as her 1936 photograph of the Prevost Players when they performed a Passion play, *The Alabaster Box*, as an Xavier University fund-raiser. But the majority of the group portraits she made were of wedding parties, such as the beautifully detailed hand-painted 1946 picture of the Lorraine McCarthy and Morris Labostrie wedding (plate 7). She also photographed the twenty members of the Iona Molizone and Laurence F. Keller wedding party. My mother, Arthé Perrault, married Flournoy Louis Anthony in 1948, and Florestine photographed their wedding party in the bride's family's living room (photo 53). To attract brides and grooms, Florestine ran ads offering to provide transportation from churches to Collins Studio.

Florestine kept pace with other black entrepreneurs by promoting her business in tribute ads marking important events such as the 1935 opening of Dillard University. She congratulated the school while offering quick-finish photographs that cost as little as ten cents and could be made "while you wait." Her ads also urged customers to enlarge old photographs. She was quick to spot an advertising opportunity such as the 1935 ten-round Wesley Farrell vs. Holman Williams World's Colored Lightweight Championship: "The Biggest Event in Crescent City History," the *Louisiana Weekly* reported. A beauty shop, beer parlor, and dentist's office also extended their best wishes to Farrell, the local favorite. Florestine's best wishes came with an offer of ten-cent photographs of the winner of the championship fight. Alas, support from Farrell's hometown crowd could not lift him to victory. He lost to Williams on a TKO in the eighth round.

Bronzed baby shoes that could be mounted on a Lucite picture frame or a heavy metal ashtray sold for $9.95 a pair at Florestine's studio. The shoes were promoted as an ideal gift for Father's Day. In addition, Collins Studio was one of several black businesses that sold tickets to public events such as performances by Fats Waller and Cab Calloway and his Cotton Club Orchestra. A big part of Rampart Street's attraction was its nightlife and the variety of adult entertainment it provided. According to the *Louisiana Weekly*, some sophisticates went "clothed pridefully in fashionable evening wear, stag[ing] their own kind of glittering social parade" to attend dances held in places such as the Pelican Gardens as well as the Astoria Hotel. National stars such as Ethel Waters, Fletcher Henderson, Nat "King" Cole, and the Mills Brothers stayed at the Astoria while performing in town. There were also far less elegant night spots in the area such as Animule Hall and the Big 25 for dancing, drinking, gambling, and prostitution. The farther south of Canal Street a business was located, the rougher the crowd.

But in the 1930s and 1940s, Florestine and her employees did not contend

Photo 53. Arthé C. Perrault and Flournoy L. Anthony wedding, 1948.

directly with the seamier side of South Rampart Street because the studio closed at 7:00 p.m. Regardless of the social distance between Florestine and Rampart's demimonde, there were many reminders close by of the desperate economic circumstances confronting the city's poor. A state Public Welfare commodity distribution office was located across the street from her studio.

Whites who owned the vast majority of the businesses and all of the property profited economically from their ability to define and maintain the racial boundaries of Rampart as a "Negro street." However, whites were free to cross those borders. As the 1938 *WPA City Guide* reassured its readers, "White persons" were admitted "at any time" to black nightclubs such as Tick Tock Tavern for "music and floor shows . . . handled in the Harlem manner—nothing less than 'red hot.'" White voyeurs and jazz aficionados went to Rampart expecting to hear music stereotypically described in the *City Guide* as having "the 'swing' that causes Negroes to move their bodies and tap their feet."

"She *Ran* the Business
and Took *Care* of Business"

As many scholars have noted, city streets were considered primarily male domains. In the context of prevailing values, Florestine's decision to relocate to South Rampart underscores her boldness as a female entrepreneur. When she opened her Rampart Street studio, she was forty years old and already had fifteen years of experience resisting traditional gender roles. Known for her professionalism and personal warmth, she was in business for herself in a period when the numbers of African American professionals in the city and state were dismally low. Clearly conscious of her high visibility, she wore a suit to work, as seen in a photograph of her in the 1930s (plate 8). She dressed like a professional woman when so many black women were forced to wear uniforms as symbols of their second-class status when working for whites.

She insisted on maintaining a businesslike atmosphere in the studio and had her female employees wear smocks to protect them from the chemicals used to make photographs. Betty Goudeau Wethers, an employee from the 1940s, remembered Florestine as "very gracious, calm, and to a point precise in what she did and what she wanted done. I honestly can't remember any admonishments, or bad moments, although I am sure they must have been there. She was a businesswoman. And when I say businesswoman, I mean she *ran* the business and she took *care* of business." She described Florestine as "a predominant figure" in the city's black business community, saying she was "a strong woman; she wasn't a pushover." Florestine's manner was one of quiet determination, a subtle but effective style. "I mean she never offended you," Wethers said. "She stuck to her guns. I must repeat that she was a businesswoman. She was the kind of businesswoman who could step on your shoes and not even ruin the shine."

Many of her employees were children of friends and acquaintances, but Valrian Burrell Montgomery, who worked in the studio in the mid-1940s, landed her job simply by walking in and asking about openings. Montgomery, an Xavier University student at the time, called Florestine "a jewel." She knew nothing of photography when she started. "I knew very little about anything, but it was a means to an end," she said, adding that the job financed her college education. In very short order, Montgomery, a brown-skinned Creole, felt as though she had become a member of Florestine's extended family.

Ambassador Andrew Young always referred to Florestine as his "aunt" because of her close friendships with his parents and several members of his family. But he felt she exploited her workers because she paid him only five dollars for a week of work, unlike a full-time employee, who was paid fifteen. That disparity led him to quit his job. Young is surely right about being paid less than a full salary when he was in his early teens.[1]

Montgomery said Florestine and her sisters did not share the prejudices of many light-skinned Creoles who disassociated themselves from darker-skinned African Americans. "They were light-skinned people," Montgomery said, "but they didn't make me feel funny or anything. We just loved each other." Montgomery nicknamed Florestine "Boss Lady" to avoid addressing her too informally as Florestine or employing the overly formal Mrs. Collins.

Behind the scenes, Boss Lady and her sisters would make Montgomery blush by teasing her with risqué humor about boyfriends. Once the shy Montgomery was thoroughly embarrassed, the sisters would break out in good-natured laughter. Florestine's rapport with her two sisters, Mildred and Thelma, and brother-in-law, Johnny Gardina, contributed to the studio's relaxed environment. Florestine was clearly "the head of the tribe," to borrow an expression from Wethers. Unofficial membership in the "tribe" was extended to many of Florestine's employees, especially the teenage girls and young women for whom she felt responsible. "You know, we were these little teenage girls, sixteen and seventeen years old, and she was looking after us, too," Phenella Perez said, adding that Florestine saw to it that the girls would get home safely every night.

Beryl Davis Davidson, who started working at the studio part-time during her senior year at Xavier Preparatory High School in 1943–44, said no one thought it was unusual or different that Florestine ran her own business. "Nobody talked about her being a woman in business," she said. "Our family did because they were so proud of her." Davidson said her Nanan, or godmother, "always talked about her being a woman in business for herself." Although Florestine's friends were proud of her accomplishments, some middle-class black people and downtown Creoles considered South Rampart Street forbidden territory because of its gambling, drinking, and prostitution. "Rampart Street has never been your best area," Davidson said, because "they had a lot of barrooms and stuff there." South

Rampart "wasn't quite as rowdy until you got farther down" past the first few blocks, she said. "But it was still not an area for a young woman to be out alone." Montgomery also remembered the street becoming "raunchy" in the blocks south of Collins Studio. "I never did go down that street," she said, "because, you know, I was a good girl."

But Rampart was not all raunchiness, and one stretch was home to an annual Easter Parade. Then, in 1939, the *Louisiana Weekly* reported that Rampart's parade rivaled the far more famous event down Harlem's Lenox Avenue. The highlight, the newspaper noted, was the presence of "hundreds of pretties . . . [who] gladdened the eyes and hearts of many masculine admirers," filling them "with pride."[2] While some women paraded on special occasions, others worked or shopped on Rampart. But the majority of the district's businesses were owned by white men catering to black men or black men renting from white landlords—Dix's Barbershop, King's Shoe Shine Parlor, Tick Tock Tavern, Polmer Tailoring, Cohen's Loan and Jewelry Company, Reiner's Pawn Shop, and Pelican Billiard Hall, all located in the first six blocks south of Canal Street and within walking distance of Collins Studio.

While South Rampart was considered taboo by some, racial segregation made it impossible to completely shield black women from the "Negro Street." Teenage girls and boys taking the bus from downtown wards to attend McDonogh No. 35 High School, for instance, walked down that street to get to the campus. Some of those same girls patronized Florestine's studio on Sunday evenings as a form of leisure when they would take the streetcar, or walk if they did not have the money, according to one woman who later had her wedding pictures made by Collins Studio in 1945. With limited choices for entertainment, she recalled going to the studio as a fun outing. The inexpensive quick-finish head shots—some of which were hand-painted for a small additional charge—were treasured and exchanged between girlfriends in the late 1930s. Almost sixty years later this same woman still had one that was taken of a friend.

With her second husband, Collins, Florestine's social life flourished because he belonged to organizations such as the Original Illinois Club, the oldest black Carnival society in New Orleans. Founded in 1895, the club introduced debutantes at its annual Mardi Gras cotillion, which did not stop during the Depression but was cancelled in 2006 in the wake of Hurricane Katrina. It returned two years later. In February 1936, the *Louisiana Weekly* described the club's ball as impressive, in part, because of its successful execution of the year's theme, "Fiesta in Old Greece," with artistic drawings on the walls, potted plants, and the tasteful use of both club and Mardi Gras colors—gold, green, and purple. All of this set the stage for the presentation of that year's debutante queen.

"Times Were Different Then"

Like virtually everything in New Orleans, Mardi Gras, the city's signature celebration, was segregated in the 1930s and 1940s. Creoles masked and paraded downtown, especially on the Claiborne Street neutral ground lined with oak trees and azaleas. Other African Americans celebrated in their neighborhoods uptown. The Mardi Gras season started after the first of the year, culminating on Mardi Gras Day, the "Fat Tuesday" before Ash Wednesday, the start of Lent, which falls in February or March. For whites, Mardi Gras Day was marked by the floats sponsored by clubs known as krewes. Except for the Zulus, who joined the main parade in 1968, the krewes were all white. From their starting point on St. Charles Avenue, the floats turned on Canal Street, where anxious crowds waited. Lolita Gonzales Belfield remembers her father taking her and one of her brothers to watch the parades, where they stood on a ladder to improve their view. Unlike today, African Americans were kept on the periphery of the parades.

Creoles and other African Americans celebrated the season with formal balls and costume parties reflecting a club's theme for the year. Florestine and Herbert would have joined the festivities sponsored by the Bunch Club and her sister Thelma's Inner Circle Bridge Club. They also went to the dances given annually by the Plantation Revelers, Thelma's husband's club. In 1941, Florestine photographed her sister Mildred with her club dressed as gypsies (photo 54). Part of the Creole tradition, Wendell Belfield said, was to visit friends' homes, often with their children. The visitors were served food—*calas*, a fried rice pastry, and donuts now called *beignets*. "Times were different then," Belfield explained. People would parade in their neighborhoods as individuals or clubs that stopped along the way for a drink at places like Belfield's Pharmacy on St. Bernard Avenue. Even though he was five or six years old at the time, Belfield still remembers the Baby Dolls club

Photo 54. Florestine's sister Mildred Gardina and her Mardi Gras Club, 1941.

in their very short skirts stopping at his father's pharmacy. Belfield's wife, Lolita, also remembered the Mardi Gras Indians parading in their elaborate headdresses and costumes. As a child, she found the Indians intriguing and frightening because of their mock tribal "wars." Florestine photographed many Mardi Gras celebrants, including her friend Mae Fuller Keller, dressed for a formal dance and leaning against a column (plate 9). Bea Duncan, also Florestine's good friend, poses holding a Spanish fan and wearing large earrings (photo 55). Mardi Gras, however, was not just for adults. In 1938, Walter and Andrew Young dressed as cowboys (photo 56).

In addition to going to Mardi Gras balls, Florestine and Herbert entertained in what the *Louisiana Weekly* described as their "luxuriously appointed" Galvez Street home by hosting, for instance, the Original Pokeno Club on a New Year's Eve. The Collinses also hosted friends such as Bobbie Anderson, whom Florestine photographed, and her husband, Bill Anderson, when they visited the South (plate 10). Hosting overnight guests was a gesture of friendship and southern-style hospitality but also a necessary courtesy because of the lack of acceptable black-owned hotels.

Photo 55. Bea Duncan,
a family friend, dressed
for Mardi Gras, early
1940s.

Florestine was photographed with celebrities such as Duke Ellington in a
group shot taken in Mag Perez's large home on Rocheblave Street (photo 57). The
Louisiana Weekly published a Bedou photograph of Florestine after she and her
husband took a monthlong vacation to the West Coast in the 1930s. The caption
read "The Lady Goes West" and described her as "the charming and popular
photographer of the city."

As reflections of the gender roles that inhibited black women from working
outside of their studios, the portraits made by Florestine did not appear in the
Louisiana Weekly nearly as often as those made by her contemporary male photographers. As Phenella Perez remembered, "I don't think she went out much

Photo 56. Walter and Andrew Young dressed as cowboys for Mardi Gras, 1938. Daisy Young Family Papers. By permission of Amistad Research Center at Tulane University.

hauling equipment; people came to the studio." She would take her equipment to her home to photograph friends who were passing for white and did not want to be seen on Rampart Street. All of Florestine's photographs appearing in the newspaper continued to be portraits of infants, children, and wedding parties. This contrasted with photographs made by Bedou and Paddio of political meetings, banquets, jazz performances, and local milestones. Despite those differences Florestine's studio was tremendously successful for almost thirty years. Given her

Photo 57. Florestine and Marguerite Perez with Duke Ellington and friends, mid-1930s. By permission of Wilbur Perez.

considerable experience and success working against and within the boundaries of her gender and race, it is highly unlikely that she lamented the fact that she worked almost exclusively in her studio.

As the eldest of her siblings, Florestine remained the head of our family in New Orleans and Los Angeles, where she moved in 1949 after retiring. No important decisions were made without soliciting her opinion and approval. She remained close to her family in New Orleans, frequently inviting them to visit. Her mother did so in 1950, and her father lived with her until he died in 1954. Florestine, whom we called Aunt Teeny, had an open door policy, according to my mother, permitting family members to live with her while they were getting established before they moved into their own homes.

Photo 58. Arthé A. Anthony, Florestine's grand-niece, at First Communion in Los Angeles, 1955.

Although she retired from the photography business, Florestine never really retired. She became a real estate investor and enjoyed enough success to help her relatives buy their first homes. She did not open a studio in Los Angeles, but she enjoyed making pictures of her family. One family photo is of me standing in front of her living room mantel in 1955, wearing my First Communion dress, holding my missal and smiling (photo 58). Even when I was young she was a fascinating person—an artist and celebrity to my naïve eyes. Her kiln in her Los Angeles garage allowed her to continue expressing her creativity as a ceramicist. Some of her work included hand-painted ashtrays shaped as reclining women, some of whom were risqué. These always intrigued me and my sister Leslie when we explored her vanity table. Florestine also created an artist's vision of a garden where she enjoyed entertaining. She grew a variety of plants including fruit trees and succulents that made her backyard a perfect setting for entertaining outdoors (photo 59).

Photo 59. Florestine Perrault Collins's backyard party in Los Angeles, 1950s.

In addition to hand-painting pottery, she found new passions and hobbies, including knitting, hat making and reupholstering furniture. She learned these skills in adult education night classes at Los Angeles's Dorsey High School near her home. Although she considered Los Angeles her home for many years after moving there in 1949, as she aged, she longed for the home where she born in 1895. She returned to New Orleans in 1975 when she was eighty years old. She wanted to be close to her family so she arranged to live with her dear friend Jeannette Warburg Altimus on Touro Street. She remained with Altimus until complications of old age made it necessary to move her to a nursing home, where she died in 1988 after a long illness.

When I embarked on the study of her career and life, what I learned about her never ceased to amaze me, especially her independence, considerable spunk, zest for life, strong will, and wicked sense of humor. She often did the unexpected, including painting the exterior of her house when she was in her sixties, and volunteering for a hotline when she was in her eighties. She had a keen sense of her world, its beauty, and its trials. She enjoyed challenges and relished her many successes. She left us a legacy of our family's past, a collective memory of our shared history.

Her photographs live to tell her story. They graphically chronicle the life and times of New Orleans's Creoles and African Americans in black and white. Florestine was keenly aware of segregation's restrictions, and she successfully negotiated the constraints of race and gender. Her reputation attracted parents who brought their babies and children to her studio. Wedding parties, high school graduates, and debutantes also came. Her skillful use of the camera allowed her to make intimate portraits of individuals and groups, starting in the early years of her career until the late 1940s. Contemporary readers can easily see that her photographs document the presence, beauty, and dignity of Creole and African American life, a world potentially forgotten especially in light of Hurricane Katrina's far-reaching devastation in 2005. No hurricane can destroy the past if the artists who lived it left a record. Florestine Perrault Collins's photographs are part of that record.

Acknowledgments

I have incurred far too many debts to be able to thank everyone who has supported me on this long journey of research and writing. Without Edward J. Boyer, this book would never have seen the light of day. I am grateful for his considerable expertise as a former editor for the *Los Angeles Times*, and his steadfast determination. I am deeply indebted to him. Funding for this project was provided by Occidental College's Louis and Hermione Brown Fund and additional grants awarded by Occidental's Deans of the College David Axeen, Eric Frank, and Jorge González; a Rockefeller Humanities Fellowship at the Center for Research on Women, University of Memphis; an Emily Schoenbaum Research Grant, Center for Research on Women, Newcomb College at Tulane University; and from the Louisiana Endowment for the Humanities.

I also benefited from participating in several summer institutes including the National Endowment for the Humanities Summer Seminar for College Teachers "Forms of Autobiography," directed by James Olney at Louisiana State University, who encouraged me from the start. My participation in the Rockefeller Humanities Fellowship "Womanist Studies Consortium," University of Georgia, and in the National Endowment for the Humanities Summer Seminar for College Teachers "Social Historians Write Biography," at the Newberry Library were important experiences as I worked to better understand Florestine Perrault Collins and how to tell her life story and impart the significance of her work.

Librarians, archivists, and curators who provided invaluable assistance include Gregory Osborn, New Orleans Public Library, Louisiana Division, who was my research assistant and friend. Brenda Square and Christopher Harter, Amistad Research Center at Tulane University; Lynn Abbott, Hogan Jazz Archive at Tulane University; and Daniel Hammer of the Historic New Orleans Collection shared photographs from their collections. I also thank Ryan Brubacher and Nancy Grubb of Occidental College and Tania Perez for their assistance.

Florestine Perrault Collins's photographs have appeared in several exhibitions including *Reflections in Black: A History of Black Photographers 1840 to the Present*, curated by Deborah Willis; *Pictures from Home: Six African American Photographers in the South, 1900 to 1950*, curated by Ellen Fleurov; *Portraits by Florestine Perrault Collins, New Orleans Photographer, 1895 to 1988*, curated by Linda Lyke; and *Florestine Perrault Collins, 1895 to 1988*, curated by Valencia Hawkins.

I had the unwavering support of my family, especially my parents, Arthé Perrault and Flournoy Louis Anthony. Many others went above and beyond the call of duty. Deborah Willis encouraged me over many years to tell "our girl's" story. She never lost faith that I would complete this project. Monique M. Taylor tirelessly read and critiqued several drafts of the manuscript. Deborah A. Martinson was a patient listener and thoughtful critic. Catherine Reinhardt and Philippe Zacaïr also helped to make this book possible. Vic and Germaine Vavasseur and Carmelita Lagarde played important roles as well. I had many supporters along the way, including Vicki Dellaverson, Raúl Fernández, Jane Jaquette, Marguerite Jones, Ray Lou, James M. Montoya, Timothy Pylko, and Gilda Sheppard. My colleague Xiao-huang Yin kept the American Studies Program at Occidental College afloat when I was on leave. I would also like to thank my editor, Amy Gorelick, for her patience and support and Patricia Brady and Bridget Cooks for their constructive comments.

My greatest debt of gratitude is owed to the New Orleanians who entrusted me with their stories for more than thirty years starting when I was a graduate student working on my dissertation under the direction of D. Dickson Bruce at the University of California, Irvine.

In some modest way this book ensures that Florestine Perrault Collins's work and life and the history of New Orleans Creoles will not be forgotten.

Notes

Chapter 2. "We Got the Hang of It"

1. Moutoussamy-Ashe, *Viewfinders*, 51.
2. *Louisiana Weekly*, 30 December 1939.
3. Ibid., 14 January 1939.
4. David Cohn, *Where I Was Born and Raised* (Boston: Houghton Mifflin, 1948), 122, quoted in Ownby, *American Dreams in Mississippi*, 79.

Chapter 3. "The Moment You're a Creole, It Was la Même Chose"

1. Blassingame, *Black New Orleans*, 11.
2. Osborn, *A Brief Family History*, 5.
3. Gould, "The Free People of Color," 41.
4. Toledano and Christovich, *New Orleans Architecture*, 187.

Chapter 4. "We Couldn't Sit in the Front"

1. DeVore and Logsdon, *Crescent City Schools*, 179.
2. Ibid., 41.
3. Ibid.
4. Albanese, *America*, 83.

Chapter 5. "She Never Went Outside One Day to Work"

1. Hair, *Carnival of Fury*, 81–82.

Chapter 6. "I Tore Out Barefooted, Running down to the Track"

1. Haas, "Bourbonism, Populism, and Little Progressivism," 223.

Chapter 7. "We Never Bothered about Sex"

1. Dumenil, *Modern Temper*, 132.

Chapter 8. "I Don't Remember Her Going Out to Any Public Places"

1. *New Orleans Herald*, 19 September 1925.
2. Gover, *The Positive Image*, 14.
3. Ibid., 17.
4. Moutoussamy-Ashe, *Viewfinders*, 19.
5. Ibid., 20; Holland, "Photography for Our Young People," 6.
6. Harris, *The Harder We Run*, 39.
7. Shaw, *What a Woman Ought to Be and Do*, 119.
8. Moutoussamy-Ashe, *Viewfinders*, 52, 60–71.
9. Birt, "A Life in American Photography," 44.
10. Hair, *Carnival of Fury*.
11. Franklin and Moss, *From Slavery to Freedom*, 317.
12. Ross, "Where Lynching Is a Habit," 627.

Chapter 9. "Photography Requires Nimble Fingers"

1. Gover, *The Positive Image,* 104–6.
2. Holland, "Photography for Our Young People," 5–9.
3. Neverdon-Morton, *Afro-American Women of the South*, 3.
4. Tate, *Domestic Allegories of Political Desire*, 151.
5. Dumenil, *The Modern Temper*, 98.
6. Ibid., 112.
7. Moutoussamy-Ashe, *Viewfinders*, 31.

Chapter 10. "Persistent Yearnings to Be Free"

1. Alain Locke, ed, *The New Negro*, with a preface by Robert Hayden (New York: Atheneum, 1969), 3.
2. Langston Hughes, *The Big Sea*, with a new introduction by Arnold Rampersad (New York: Hill and Wang, 1993), 228.
3. Wall, *Louisiana: A History*, 235.
4. Tyler, *Silk Stockings and Ballot Boxes*, 21, 23, 26–27.
5. Ibid., 27.
6. Hine, *Hine Sight*, 9.
7. Fairclough, *Race and Democracy*, 23
8. Ibid., 18–19.
9. *Civic Leader (A Magazine for the Better Kind),* June 1929, A. P. Tureaud Papers, Amistad Research Center, Tulane University.
10. Ibid., October-November 1929, 5, A. P. Tureaud Papers, Amistad Research Center, Tulane University.
11. Logsdon and Cossé Bell, "The Americanization of Black New Orleans," 234–35.
12. Dumenil, *Freemasonry and American Culture*, 161.
13. Ibid., 49.

Chapter 11. Three Prominent Creole Photographers

1. *Louisiana Weekly,* 24 March 1934, NOPL, LD.

2. Rosenblum, *A History of Women Photographers*, 109.

3. Ibid., 150.

4. Ibid., 151.

5. Gover, *The Positive Image,* 46.

6. Ausherman, *The Photographic Legacy of Frances Benjamin Johnston*, 12.

7. Gover, *The Positive Image,* 53.

8. Ibid., 85.

9. Federal Works Project, *New Orleans City Guide,* American Guide Series, 107.

10. Trachtenberg, *Reading American Photographs*, 165.

Chapter 12. "I Met Herbert and Fell in Love with Him"

1. Govenar, *Portraits of Community*, 30.

2. Willis "Picturing the New Negro Woman," 227–43.

3. Gaines, *Uplifting the Race*, 67.

4. Ibid., 68–69.

Chapter 13. "Everybody Got All Dressed Up and Went to the Studio"

1. www.ms.com/winter2004/jazz.asp.

2. Gregory Osborn, e-mail message to author, 8 March 2010.

3. Moutoussamy-Ashe, *Viewfinders*, 136.

4. *Louisiana Weekly,* 24 March 1934.

5. Clark, *Delta Shadows*, 125.

6. *Louisiana Weekly*, 15 February 1936 and 23 October 1937.

7. Kuh, Joye, and West, *Living Atlanta*, 37.

8. Ibid., 39.

Chapter 15. "She *Ran* the Business and Took *Care* of Business"

1. Young, *An Easy Burden*, 39.

2. *Louisiana Weekly*, 15 April 1939.

Bibliography

Interviews by the Author

Altimus, Jeanette Warburg. New Orleans. 12 December 1977, 23 July 1992, and 14 August 1992.
Anthony, Arthé Perrault. Los Angeles. 12 July 2001.
Belfield, Wendell, and Lolita Gonzales Belfield. Telephone interview. 11 August 2010.
Cavanaugh, Enola. New Orleans. 3 March 1977.
Chevalier, Alice Simon, and Everett Chevalier. New Orleans. 21 February 1977.
Collins, Florestine Perrault. Los Angeles. 17 March 1975.
Davidson, Beryl Davis. Los Angeles. 6 July 1994.
Holland, Theresa. New Orleans. 1 December 1977.
Labat, Yvonne Johnson. New Orleans. 20 February 1977.
Mckenna, George, Sr., New Orleans. 15 March 1977.
Meteye, Judith Fluger, and Robert Meteye Sr. New Orleans. 15 February 1977.
Montgomery, Valrian Burrell. New Orleans. 28 February 2000.
Moore, Gaston F., Sr., New Orleans. 1 April 1977.
Perez, Marguerite Montegut, and Bertha Montegut Tate. New Orleans. 17 February 1977.
Perez, Phenella DuPlessis. Los Angeles. 8 July 1993.
Perrault, Gladys Williams. Los Angeles. 2 May 1975.
Prevost, Eva Jamet. New Orleans. 16 November 1977.
Sindos, Lydia Gumbel. New Orleans. 15 February 1977.
Taylor, Marceline Bucksell. Interview by the author and Lloyd Gonzales. New Orleans. 16 March 1977.
Wethers, Betty Goudeau. Los Angeles. 22 June 1995.
Young, Andrew, Sr., New Orleans. 26 February 1977.

Other Sources

Aackley, E. Azalia. *The Colored Girl Beautiful*. Chicago: n.p., 1916.
Albanese, Catherine L. *America: Religions and Religion*. Belmont, Calif.: Wadsworth, 1992.
Alexander, Adele Logan. *Ambiguous Lives: Free Women of Color in Rural Georgia, 1789–1879*. Fayetteville: University of Arkansas Press, 1991.

Anderson, Kent. *Woman of Color, Daughter of Privilege*. Athens: University of Georgia Press, 1995.

Anthony, Arthé. "Florestine Perrault Collins and the Gendered Politics of Black Portraiture in 1920s New Orleans." *Louisiana History* 2 (Spring 2002).

———. "'Lost Boundaries': Racial Passing and Poverty in Segregated New Orleans." In *Creole: The History and Legacy of Louisiana's Free People of Color,* edited by Sybil Kein, 295–316. Baton Rouge: Louisiana State University Press, 2000. Previously published in *Louisiana History* 36 (Summer 1995).

———. "The Negro Creole Community in New Orleans, 1880s–1920s: An Oral History." Ph.D. diss., University of California, Irvine, 1978.

Arnesen, Eric. *Waterfront Workers of New Orleans: Race, Class and Politics, 1863–1923*. New York: Oxford University Press, 1991.

Ausherman, Maria Elizabeth. *The Photographic Legacy of Frances Benjamin Johnston*. Gainesville: University Press of Florida, 2009.

Baker, Tracey. "Nineteenth-Century Minnesota Women Photographers." *Journal of the West* 28 (1989).

Beardsley, Edward H. *A History of Neglect: Health Care for Blacks and Mill Workers in the Twentieth Century*. Knoxville: University of Tennessee Press, 1987.

Bell, Caryn Cossé. *Revolution, Romanticism, and the Afro-Creole Protest Tradition in Louisiana, 1718–1868*. Baton Rouge: Louisiana State University Press, 1997.

Bennett, James B. "Catholics, Creoles and the Definition of Race in New Orleans." In *Race Nation, and Religion in the Americas,* edited by Henry Goldschmidt and Elizabeth McAlister. New York: Oxford University Press, 2004.

Berlin, Ira. Slaves *without Masters: The Free Negro of the Antebellum South*. New York: Vintage, 1976.

Birken, Lawrence. *Consuming Desire: Sexual Science and the Emergence of a Culture of Abundance, 1871–1914*. Ithaca: Cornell University Press, 1988.

Birt, Rodger C. "A Life in American Photography." In *VanDerZee, Photographer, 1886–1983*, edited by Deborah Willis-Braithwaite. Washington, D.C.: Harry N. Abrams, in association with National Portrait Gallery, Smithsonian Institution, in conjunction with the exhibition *James VanDerZee Photographer 1886–1983* at the National Portrait Gallery, Smithsonian Institution, Washington, D.C., 1993.

Blassingame, John. *Black New Orleans, 1860–1880*. Chicago: University of Chicago, 1973.

Brady, Patricia. "Black Artists in Antebellum New Orleans." *Louisiana History* 32 (1991): 5–28.

Brasseux, Carl A., Keith P. Fontenot, and Claude F. Oubre. *Creoles of the Bayou Country*. Jackson: University Press of Mississippi, 1994.

Bronson, Charlotte. "Because I Am a Woman." *Life and Labor* 10 (1920): 173–74.

Brown, Elsa Barkley. "'What Has Happened Here': The Politics of Difference in Women's History and Feminist Politics." *Feminist Studies* 18 (Summer 1992): 295–312.

Broyard, Bliss. *One Drop: My Father's Hidden Life*. New York: Little, Brown, 2007.

Bryant, Violet Harrington. *The Myth of New Orleans in Literature: Dialogues of Race and Gender*. Knoxville: University of Tennessee Press, 1993.

Campbell, Mary Schmidt. Introduction to *Harlem Renaissance: Art of Black America*. New York: Studio Museum in Harlem with Harry N. Abrams, 1987.

Clark, Peter Wellington, comp. *Delta Shadows: A Pageant of Negro Progress in New Orleans*. New Orleans: Graphic Arts Studio, 1942.

Cochran, Robert. *A Photographer of Note: Arkansas Artist Gleeve Grice*. Fayetteville: University of Arkansas Press, 2003.

Corrales, Barbara Smith. "Parlors, Politics, and Privilege: Clubwomen and the Failure of Woman Suffrage in Lafayette, Louisiana, 1897–1922." *Louisiana History* 38 (1997).

Crouch, Stanley. *One Shot Harris: The Photographs of Charles "Teenie" Harris*. New York: Harry N. Abrams.

Davidov, Judith Fryer. "Containment and Excess: Representing African Americans." Chapter 4 of *Women's Camera Work: Self/Body/Other in American Visual History*. Durham: Duke University Press, 1998.

Davis, Cyprian. *The History of Black Catholics in the United States*. New York: Crossroads, 1992.

De Cock, Liliane, and Reginald McGhee, eds. *James Van Der Zee*. 1973. New Brunswick, N.J.: Rutgers University Press, 1986.

Deppen, Grace R. "Photography for Women." *Photo Era*, August 1922.

Desdunes, Rodolph Lucien. *Our People and Our History*. Translated and edited by Sister Dorothea Olga McCants. Baton Rouge: Louisiana State University Press, 1973.

DeVore, Donald E., and Joseph Logsdon, eds. *Crescent City Schools: Publication Education in New Orleans, 1841–1991*. Lafayette: Center for Louisiana Studies, 1991.

Dominguez, Virginia. *White by Definition: Social Classification in Creole Louisiana*. New Brunswick, N.J.: Rutgers University Press, 1986.

Driskell, David C. *Two Centuries of Black American Art*. New York: Los Angeles County Museum of Art and Knopf, 1976.

Dumenil, Lynn. *Freemasonry and American Culture, 1880–1930*. Princeton: Princeton University Press, 1984.

———. *The Modern Temper: American Culture and Society in the 1920s*. New York: Hill and Wang, 1995.

Ehrenreich, Barbara, and Deirdre English. *For Her Own Good: 150 Years of the Experts' Advice to Women*. Garden City, N.J.: Anchor, 1979.

Ellis, Havelock. *Studies in the Psychology of Sex*. Philadelphia: F. A. Davis, 1908.

Fairclough, Adam. *Race and Democracy: The Civil Rights Struggle in Louisiana, 1915–1972*. Athens: University of Georgia Press, 1995.

Federal Writers' Project of the Works Progress Administration for the City of New Orleans. *New Orleans City Guide*. American Guide Series. Cambridge, Mass.: Riverside Press, 1938.

Fernández, Raúl. *Latin Jazz: The Perfect Combination*. San Francisco: Chronicle Books in association with the Smithsonian Institution, 2002.

Fiehrer, Thomas. *Louisiana's Black Heritage*, edited by Robert R. McDonald, John R. Kemp, and Edward F. Haas. New Orleans: Louisiana State Museum, 1979.

———. "Saint-Domingue/Haiti: Louisiana's Caribbean Connection." *Louisiana History* 30 (1989): 419–37.

Fischer, Robert A. *The Segregation Struggle in Louisiana, 1862–77*. Urbana: University of Illinois Press, 1974.

Flucker, Turry, and Phoenix Savage. *Images of America: African Americans in New Orleans*. Charleston: Arcadia, 2010.

Foner, Laura. "The Free People of Color in Louisiana and St. Domingue: A Comparative Portrait of Two Three-Caste Slave Societies." *Journal of Social History* 3 (1970): 406–30.

Franklin, John Hope, and Alfred A. Moss Jr. *From Slavery to Freedom: A History of Negro Americans*. 6th ed. New York: Knopf, 1988.

Gaines, Kevin J. *Uplifting the Race: Black Leadership, Politics and Culture in the Twentieth Century*. Chapel Hill: University of North Carolina Press, 1996.

Gillard, John T. *The Catholic Church and the American Negro*. 1929. Reprint, New York: Johnson Reprint Corp., 1968.

Goings, Kenneth W. *Mammy and Uncle Mose: Black Collectibles and American Stereotyping*. Bloomington: Indiana University Press, 1994.

Gordon, Louise. *Caste & Class: The Black Experience in Arkansas, 1880–1920*. Athens: University of Georgia Press, 1995.

Gould, Virginia Meacham. "The Free People of Color of the Antebellum Gulf Ports of Mobile and Pensacola: The Struggle for a Middle Ground." In *Creoles of Color of the Gulf South*, edited by James H. Dormon. Knoxville: University of Tennessee Press, 1996.

Govenar, Alan. *Portraits of Community: African Americans in Texas*. Austin: State Historical Society, 1996.

Gover, C. Jane. *The Positive Image: Women Photographers in Turn of the Century America*. Albany: State University of New York Press, 1988.

Haas, Edward F. "Bourbonism, Populism, and Little Progressivism, 1892–1924." In *Louisiana, A History*, 3rd ed., edited by Bennett H. Wall et al. Wheeling, Ill.: Harlan Davidson, 1997.

Hair, William Ivy. *Carnival of Fury: Robert Charles and the New Orleans Race Riot of 1900*. Baton Rouge: Louisiana State University Press, 1976.

Hall, Gwendolyn Midlo. *Africans in Colonial Louisiana: The Development of Afro-Creole Culture in the Eighteenth Century*. Baton Rouge: Louisiana State University Press, 1992.

Hanger, Kimberly S. *Bounded Lives, Bounded Places: Free Black Society in Colonial New Orleans 1769–1803*. Durham: Duke University Press, 1997.

———. "Origins of New Orleans's Free People of Color." In *Creoles of Color of the Gulf South*, edited by James H. Dormon. Knoxville: University of Tennessee Press, 1996.

Harris, William H. *The Harder We Run: Black Workers since the Civil War*. New York: Oxford University Press, 1982.

Hart, Sister Mary Francis Borgia, S.S.F. *Violets in the King's Garden: A History of the Sisters of the Holy Family*. New Orleans: n.p., 1976.

Haskins, Jim. *James VanDerZee: The Picture-Takin' Man*. Trenton: Africa World Press, 1991.

Hickman, R. C. *Behold the People: R. C Hickman's Photographs of Black Dallas, 1949–1961*. Austin: Center for American History by the Texas State Historical Association, 1994.

Hine, Darlene Clark. "Black Migration to the Midwest: The Gender Dimension, 1914–45." In *The Great Migration in Historical Perspective*, edited by Joe Trotter Jr. Bloomington: University of Indiana Press, 1991.

———. *Black Women in White: Racial Conflict and Cooperation in the Nursing Profession, 1890–1950*. Bloomington: Indiana University Press, 1989.

———. *Hine Sight: Black Womanhood and the Reconstruction of American History*. Bloomington: Indiana University Press, 1994.

Hirsch, Arnold R., and Joseph Logsdon. *Creole New Orleans: Race and Americanization*. Baton Rouge: Louisiana State University Press, 1992.

Hirsch, Julia. *Family Photographs: Content, Meaning and Effect*. New York: Oxford University Press, 1981.

Holland, W. W. "Photography for Our Young People." *Colored American Magazine*, 1902.

Hollandsworth, James G. *The Louisiana Native Guards: The Black Military Experience during the Civil War*. Baton Rouge: Louisiana State University Press, 1995.

Ingham, John H. "Patterns of African-American Female Self-Employment and Entrepreneurship in Ten Southern Cities." Paper presented at the Tenth Berkshire Conference on the History of Women, Chapel Hill, North Carolina, 6 June 1996.

Johnson, Thomas L., and Philip C. Dunn, eds. *A True Likeness: The Black South of Richard Samuel Roberts, 1920–1936*. Columbia S.C.: Broccoli Clark; Chapel Hill: Algonquin Books of Chapel Hill, 1986.

Jones, Jacqueline. *Labor of Love, Labor of Sorrow: Black Women, Work, and the Family from Slavery to the Present*. New York: Basic, 1985.

Kein, Sybil, ed. *Creole: The History and Legacy of Louisiana's Free People of Color*. Baton Rouge: Louisiana State University Press, 2000.

Kuh, Clifford M., Harlon E. Joye, and E. Bernard West. *Living Atlanta: An Oral History of the City, 1914–1948*. Atlanta: Atlanta Historical Society; Athens: University of Georgia, 1990.

Kunpfer, Anne Meis. *Toward a Tenderer Humanity and a Nobler Womanhood: African American Women's Clubs in Turn-of-the-Century Chicago*. New York: New York University Press, 1996.

LaChance, Paul. F. "The 1809 Immigration of Saint-Domingue Refugees to New Orleans: Reception, Integration and Impact." *Louisiana History* 29 (1988): 109–41.

Levey, Jane Freudel. "The Scurlock Studio." In *Visual Journal: Harlem and D.C. in the Thirties and Forties*, edited by Deborah Willis and Jane Lusaka. Washington, D.C.: Center for African American History and Culture and Smithsonian Institution Press, 1996.

Lewis, David Levering, and Deborah Willis. *A Small Nation of People: W.E.B. Du Bois and African American Portraits of Progress*. Washington D.C.: Library of Congress, 2003.

Logsdon, Joseph, and Caryn Cossé Bell. "The Americanization of Black New Orleans." In *Creole New Orleans: Race and Americanization*, edited by Arnold Hirsch and Joseph Logsdon. Baton Rouge: Louisiana State University Press, 1992.

Long, Alecia P. *The Great Southern Babylon: Sex, Race, and Respectability in New Orleans, 1865–1920*. Baton Rouge: Louisiana State University Press, 2004.

May, Elaine Tyler. *Great Expectations: Marriage & Divorce in Post-Victorian America*. Chicago: University of Chicago Press, 1983.

McConnell, Roland C. *Negro Troops of Antebellum Louisiana: A History of the Battalion of Free Men of Color*. Baton Rouge: Louisiana State University Press, 1968.

McDaris, Wendy, ed. *Visualizing the Blues: Images of the American South*. Published as a complement to the exhibition *Visualizing the Blues: Images of the American South, 1862–1999*. Memphis: Dixon Gallery and Gardens, 2002.

———. *Visualizing the Blues*. Memphis: Dixon Gallery and Gardens, 2000. Published in conjunction with the exhibition *Visualizing the Blues: Images of the American South, 1862–1999* at the Dixon Gallery and Gardens.

Miller, Zane L. "Urban Blacks in the South, 1865–1920: Savannah, New Orleans, Louisville and Birmingham Experience." In *The New Urban History: Quantitative Explorations by American Historians*, edited by Leo F. Schnore. Princeton: Princeton University Press, 1975.

Mills, Gary B. *The Forgotten People: Cane River's Creoles of Color*. Baton Rouge: Louisiana State University Press, 1977.

Mouton, Girard, and Tribune Staff. "The Way We Were: Our Family Album." *Tribune* 4 (July 1988).

Moutoussamy-Ashe, Jeanne. *Viewfinders: Black Women Photographers*. New York: Writers and Readers Publishing, 1993.

Neverdon-Morton, Cynthia. *Afro-American Women of the South and the Advancement of the Race, 1895–1925*. Knoxville: University of Tennessee Press, 1989.

Ochs, Stephen J. *Desegregating the Altar: The Josephites and the Struggle for Black Priests, 1871–1960*. Baton Rouge: Louisiana State University Press, 1990.

Osborn, Gregory. *A Brief Family History*. Prepared for the Perrault Family Reunion, 1996.

Osborne, Linda Barrett, ed. *A Small Nation of People: W.E.B. Du Bois and African American Portraits of Progress*. New York: Amistad; Harper Collins, 2003.

Ownby, Ted. *American Dreams in Mississippi: Consumers, Poverty & Culture: 1830–1998*. Chapel Hill: University of North Carolina Press, 1999.

Perry, Regina A. *Free within Ourselves: African-American Artists*. Washington, D.C.: National Museum of American Art and the Smithsonian Institution, 1992.

Piper, Adrian. "Passing for White, Passing for Black." *Transition* 58 (1992): 4–32.

Pitman, Barbara (Barb). "Culture, Caste, and Conflict in New Orleans Catholicism: Archbishop Francis Janssens and the Color Line." *Louisiana History* 49 (Fall 2008): 423–62.

Reynolds, Gary A., and Beryl J. Wright. *Against the Odds: African-American Artists and the Harmon Foundation*. Newark, N.J.: Newark Museum, 1989.

Rodgrique, Jessie M. "The Black Community and the Birth Control Movement." In *Passion and Power: Sexuality in History*, edited by Kathy Peiss and Christina Simmons. Philadelphia: Temple University Press, 1989.

Rose, Al. *Storyville, New Orleans: Being an Authentic, Illustrated Account of the Notorious Red-Light District*. Tuscaloosa: University of Alabama Press, 1974.

Rosenblum, Naomi. *A History of Women Photographers*. New York: Abeville Press, 1994.

Ross, Mary. "Where Lynching Is a Habit." *Survey: Midmonthly* 49 (15 February 1923).

Saunders, Doris E., comp. *Special Moments in African-American History: 1955–1966: The Photographs of Moneeta Sleet, Jr., Ebony Magazine's Pulitzer Prize Winner*. Chicago: Johnson Publishing, 1998.

Schafer, Judith K. *Slavery, the Civil Law, and the Supreme Court of Louisiana*. Baton Rouge: University of Louisiana Press, 1994.

Shaw, Stephanie J. *What a Woman Ought to Be and Do: Black Professional Women Workers during the Jim Crow Era*. Chicago: University of Chicago Press, 1996.

Simmons, John K., and Brian Wilson. *Competing Visions of Paradise: The California Experience of Nineteenth-Century American Sectarianism*. Vol. 2, *The Religious Contours of California, Window to the World's Religions*. Santa Barbara: Fithian Press, 1993.

Simpson, Anne Key. "Camile Lucille Nickerson: 'The Louisiana Lady.'" *Louisiana History* 36 (Fall 1995): 431–51.

Smith, Shawn Michelle. *Photography on the Color Line: W.E.B. Du Bois, Race, and Visual Culture*. A John Hope Franklin Center Book. Durham: Duke University Press, 2004.

Soards' New Orleans City Directory, 1913–49.

Sterkx, Henry E. *The Free Negro in Antebellum Louisiana*. Rutherford, N.J.: Fairleigh Dickinson University Press, 1972.

Tate, Claudia. *Domestic Allegories of Political Desire: The Black Heroine's Text at the Turn of the Century*. New York: Oxford University Press, 1992.

Taulbert, Clifton L. *Once upon a Time When We Were Colored*. Tulsa: Council Oak Books, 1989.

Tentler, Alice Woodcock. *Wage-Earning Women: Industrial Work and Family in the United States, 1900–1930*. New York: Oxford University Press, 1979.

Thompson, Shirley Elizabeth. *Exiles at Home: The Struggle to Become American in Creole New Orleans*. Cambridge: Harvard University Press, 2009.

Tindall, George B. *The Emergence of the New South, 1913–1945*. Baton Rouge: Louisiana State University Press, 1967.

Toledano, Roulhac, and Mary Louise Christovich. *Faubourg Tremé and the Bayou Road*. Vol. 6, *New Orleans Architecture*. Gretna, La.: Pelican, 1980.

Trachtenberg, Alan. *Reading American Photographs: Images as History, Mathew Brady to Walker Evans*. New York: Hill and Wang, Noonday Press, 1989.

Turner, Patricia A. *Ceramic Uncles & Celluloid Mammies: Black Images and Their Influence on Culture*. New York: Anchor, 1994.

Twomey, Dannehl. "Into the Mainstream: Early Black Photography in Houston." *Houston Review* 9 (1987).

Tyler, Pamela. *Silk Stockings and Ballot Boxes: Women and Politics in New Orleans, 1920–1963*. Athens: University of Georgia Press, 1996.

Vincent, Charles. *A Centennial History of Southern University and A&M College, 1880–1991*. Baton Rouge: Louisiana State University Press, 1981.

Wall, Bennett H., et al. *Louisiana: A History*. 3rd ed. Wheeling, Ill.: Harlan Davidson, 1990.

White, Shane, and Graham White. "*Stylin': African American Expressive Culture from Its Beginnings to the Zoot Suit*. Ithaca: Cornell University Press, 1998.

Wilcox, Jerry, and Anthony V. Margavio. "Occupational Representation by Race, Ethnicity and Residence in Turn-of-the-Century New Orleans." *Social Science Journal* 24 (1987): 1–16.

Willet, Mabel Hurd. *The Employment of Women in the Clothing Trade*. 1902. Reprint, New York: AMS Press, 1968.

Willis, Deborah. "Picturing the New Negro Woman." *In Black Womanhood: Images, Icons, and Ideologies of the African Body*, edited by Barbara Thompson. Hanover: Hood Museum of Art, Dartmouth College, in association with University of Washington Press, Seattle, 2008.

———. "The New Negro Image, 1900–1930." Chapter 2 of *Reflections in Black: A History of Black Photographers, 1840 to the Present*. New York: Norton, 2000.

———. *The Scurlock Studio and Black Washington: Picturing the Promise*. Washington, D.C.: National Museum of African American History and Culture in collaboration with the National Museum of American History, 2009.

———. "A Search for Self: The Photograph and Black Family Life." In *The Familial Gaze*, edited by Marianne Hirsch. Hanover: Dartmouth College, 2008. In conjunction with the exhibition *Black Womanhood: Images, Icons, and Ideologies of the African Body*, at the Hood Museum of Art, Davis Museum and Cultural Center, and San Diego Museum of Art, 2008.

Willis-Braithwaite, Deborah. "They Knew Their Names." In *VanDerZee Photographer 1886–1983*, edited by Willis-Braithwaite. Washington D.C.: Harry N. Abrams, in association with National Portrait Gallery, Smithsonian Institution. Published in conjunction with the exhibition *James VanDerZee Photographer 1886–1983* at the National Portrait Gallery, Smithsonian Institution, Washington, D.C., 1993.

Willis-Thomas, Deborah. *Black Photographers, 1840–1940: A Bio-Bibliography*. New York: Garland, 1985.

Woods, Allen T. *Woods Directory: Being a Colored Business, Professional and Trades Directory of New Orleans, Louisiana*. New Orleans: Allen T. Woods, 1913.

———. *Woods Directory: Being a Colored Business, Professional and Trades Directory of New Orleans, Louisiana*. New Orleans: Allen T. Woods, 1914.

Yans-McLaughlin, Virginia. *Family and Community*. Ithaca: Cornell University Press, 1971.

Young, Andrew. *An Easy Burden: The Civil Rights Movement and the Transformation of America*. New York: HarperCollins, 1996.

Index

Arthé A. Anthony is professor emerita of American studies at Occidental College, Los Angeles.